LĒVO

Inspired Infusions
Elevated Edibles

Cooking with LĒVO

Contents

Introduction	4
Infusing 101	6
Basic Infusions	9
Coconut Oil Infusion	10
Olive Oil Infusion	11
Butter Infusion	12
Milk or Coconut Milk Infusion	13
Rise & Shine	14
Blueberry Muffins	19
Coconut Almond Protein Balls	21
Vegan Chocolate Chip Banana Bread	23
Chia Pudding	25
Fancy Scrambled Eggs with Truffles	27
Let's Get this Party Starters	27
Guac	33
Vegan Ceviche	35
Hasselback Potato	37
Creamy Lemon Zucchini Orzo	39
Garlic Cauli-Bites	41
Pajeon (Korean Scallion Pancake)	43

Main Strains — 44

Curried Chicken Thighs	49
Watermelon Togarashi Salad	51
Ratatouille	53
Mac & Cheese & Veg	55
The Only Roast Chicken You'll Ever Need	57

The Munchies — 58

Toll in the House Cookies	63
White Chocolate Cheesecake	65
Power Gummies	67
Coconut Apricot Nugs	69

Get Your Fixins — 70

The Basic B	72
Frenchy Vinaigrette	73
Fat-Washed Cocktails	76
Old Fashioned	77
Martini	77

LĒVO

The Taste of Infusion, Uplifted.

INTRODUCTION

"There has to be a better way."

That's what LĒVO CEO Chrissy Bellman thought in 2011 while watching a group of friends struggle to infuse oil in a small apartment. It was the all-too-familiar sight and smell of edible experiments gone wrong.

Add to that Chrissy's devotion to at-home wellness, stir in years of development and design, mix in tens of thousands of imaginative LĒVO users, blend in one global pandemic, and... Voila! Ten years after Chrissy's light bulb moment, LĒVO continues to elevate the craft of kitchen counter herbal creations.

This is a cookbook written for fans: Fans of cooking. Fans of herbs. Fans of wellness. Fans of bringing new twists to proven recipes. And yes, fans of LĒVO, the premium home infuser made for infüsiasts like you. Ensure that your butter's better; that you don't spoil your oil; that you unleash delicious possibility with every batch of infused herbs, without the time or mess of traditional methods.

Some of these recipes are our own. Some were contributed by real LĒVO users. Others are recipes inspired by well-known cooking enthusiasts and seasoned chefs.

All of them promise good, clean, sense-pleasing kitchen fun. Whether you're into flower for medicine, recreation, both or neither, you'll find spirit and taste infused into every drop. LĒVO turns prose into poetry by uplifting the taste and quality of any recipe that calls for oil or butter.

They say that the difference between an amateur and a pro is the size of the waste bin. At LĒVO, our bins have gotten smaller as our infusion and cooking prowess has grown stronger. LĒVO transforms the food you create and share with friends and family, making every one of those meals a bit more magical with each blend, chop, boil, or bite.

From our LĒVO to yours, we're happy to say that there is a better way. And it starts in the pages that follow, shared by infusion enthusiasts for the infüsiast in you – new, novice, or connoisseur.

So without further adieu, put your chef's hat and apron on, get your flower and herbs ready, plug your LĒVO in, turn on some music, and get cooking.

Infusing 101

Goodbye, sticky pots. Hello, lovely oils, butters, and much more...

After you unpack your LĒVO, read the instructions, and give your accessories a quick wash, check out the Time and Temperature Calculator on LĒVO's website (levooil.com/calculator). It tells you the right temperature and length of time to infuse, depending on your herb and base of choice.

For the base of your first infusion, start with oil or butter, but don't limit yourself. As you'll see in the pages that follow, you can infuse honey, and even vinegars, too!

When the LĒVO is prepped, add your base, then program the time and temperature. Then, to quote what is perhaps the most famous late night shopping tagline of all time, "set it and forget it."

A quick note on potency

The ratio of flower to base and your tolerance are the two biggest factors in how much of a high you'll feel from any given recipe.

For most of the recipes, we used a ratio of 4 grams of flower to 1 cup of base. The best advice we have here is to experiment and sample. Longer infusion times typically result in a stronger flavor and dosage — but be aware of the temperature as some herbs and oils react better to lower temperature.

Note that the oil or butter doesn't need a green hue to be potent. If you want an additional kick with any recipe, drizzle on a bit of extra infused oil or honey, or spread with infused butter, before serving.

8

Basic Infusions

For each infusion, pack the LĒVO herb pod with your fresh botanicals of choice, or coarsely ground dried versions. Some of these recipes call for infusing with particular ingredients such as garlic, cinnamon sticks, curry spices, toasted pistachios, and more — but as always, feel free to experiment!

That said, note that too fine of a grind and your herbs will leak out of the pod; too coarse and you'll miss out on maximum infusion. After infusing, use your LĒVO herb press to infuse every last drop. Store in an airtight container or freeze into cubes using your LĒVO herb blocks. The herb press, herb blocks and many more incredible accessories are available on the LĒVO website at levooil.com.

The amount of time you want to infuse will vary based on your herbs, so be sure to reference the time and temperature calculator at levooil.com/calculator.

BASIC INFUSIONS

Coconut Oil Infusion

1. Pack LĒVO herb pod with your herb of choice. Use fresh herbs or coarsely ground dried herbs. Too finely ground and your herb will seep through into your infusion, so grind just enough to increase surface area and maximize infusion.

2. Add LĒVO herb pod into the reservoir.

3. Measure 16 oz (2 cups) of coconut oil. Don't worry if your oil is solid. (Pro tip: Use a kitchen scale lined with parchment paper to measure easily and accurately.)

4. Scoop the coconut oil into your LĒVO reservoir and close the lid.

5. Set your LĒVO to 160-175°F and infuse for 60-120 minutes, depending on your herb choice. Use the time and temperature calculator at levooil.com/calculator to be precise.

6. While the coconut oil is still warm, dispense your infusion into an airtight container. We love reusable glass jars. Use your Herb Press to dispense efficiently and get every last drop.

7. Keep your coconut oil infusion in your pantry or refrigerator. Or, for maximum freshness, keep your infusions organized and accessible by pouring them into freezer-safe Herb Blocks.

8. Savory or sweet, whatever you're cookin' up, add the flavor and health benefits of herbs with LĒVO infused coconut oil.

BASIC INFUSIONS

Olive Oil Infusion

1. Pack LĒVO herb pod with your herb of choice. Use fresh herbs or coarsely ground dried herbs. Too finely ground and your herb will seep through into your infusion, so grind just enough to increase surface area and maximize infusion.

2. Add LĒVO herb pod into the reservoir.

3. Measure up to 16 oz (2 cups) of olive oil, and add it to the reservoir. Make sure the herbs inside the Herb Pod are fully submerged in the oil.

4. Set your LĒVO to 160-175°F and infuse for 60-180 minutes, depending on your herb choice. Use the time and temperature calculator at levooil.com/calculator to be precise.

5. When the Infuse cycle is completed, dispense your infusion into a clean, airtight container. We love reusable glass jars. Use the Herb Press accessory after dispensing to get every last drop from your soaked herbs inside the Herb Pod.

6. Keep your olive oil infusion in your pantry or refrigerator. Or, for maximum freshness, keep your infusions organized and accessible by pouring them into our freezer-safe Herb Blocks storage solution.

BASIC INFUSIONS

Butter Infusion

1. Pack the herb pod using fresh or coarsely ground dried herbs. Too finely ground and your herb will seep through into your infusion, so grind just enough to increase surface area.

2. Add LĒVO herb pod into the reservoir.

3. Slice 16 oz (four sticks) of butter into large pieces so they fit nicely into the reservoir.

4. Place the butter into your reservoir and close the lid.

5. Set your LĒVO to 160-175°F and infuse for 30-120 minutes, depending on your herb choice. Use the time and temperature calculator at levooil.com/calculator to be precise.

6. While the milk is still warm, dispense your infusion into an airtight container, such as a reusable glass jar. Use your Herb Press to strain as efficiently as possible and ensure you get every last drop of the infusion.

7. Store your infused butter in the refrigerator. Or make it last longer and keep your infusions organized and accessible by pouring them into freezer-safe Herb Blocks.

BASIC INFUSIONS

Milk or Coconut Milk Infusion

1. Pack the herb pod using fresh or coarsely ground dried herbs. Don't overpack the herbs - you always want your base to move freely through the packed pod. Too finely ground and your herb will seep through into your infusion, so grind or chop just enough to increase surface area.

2. Add LĒVO herb pod into the reservoir.

3. Add 16 oz (2 cups) of milk into your reservoir and close the lid.

4. Set your LĒVO to 175-185°F and infuse for 30-150 minutes, depending on your herb choice. Use the time and temperature calculator at levooil.com/calculator to be precise.

5. While the milk is still warm, dispense your infusion into an airtight container, such as a reusable glass jar. Use your Herb Press to strain as efficiently as possible and ensure you get every last drop of the infusion.

6. Store your infused milk in the refrigerator. Or make it last longer and keep your infusions organized and accessible by pouring them into freezer-safe Herb Blocks.

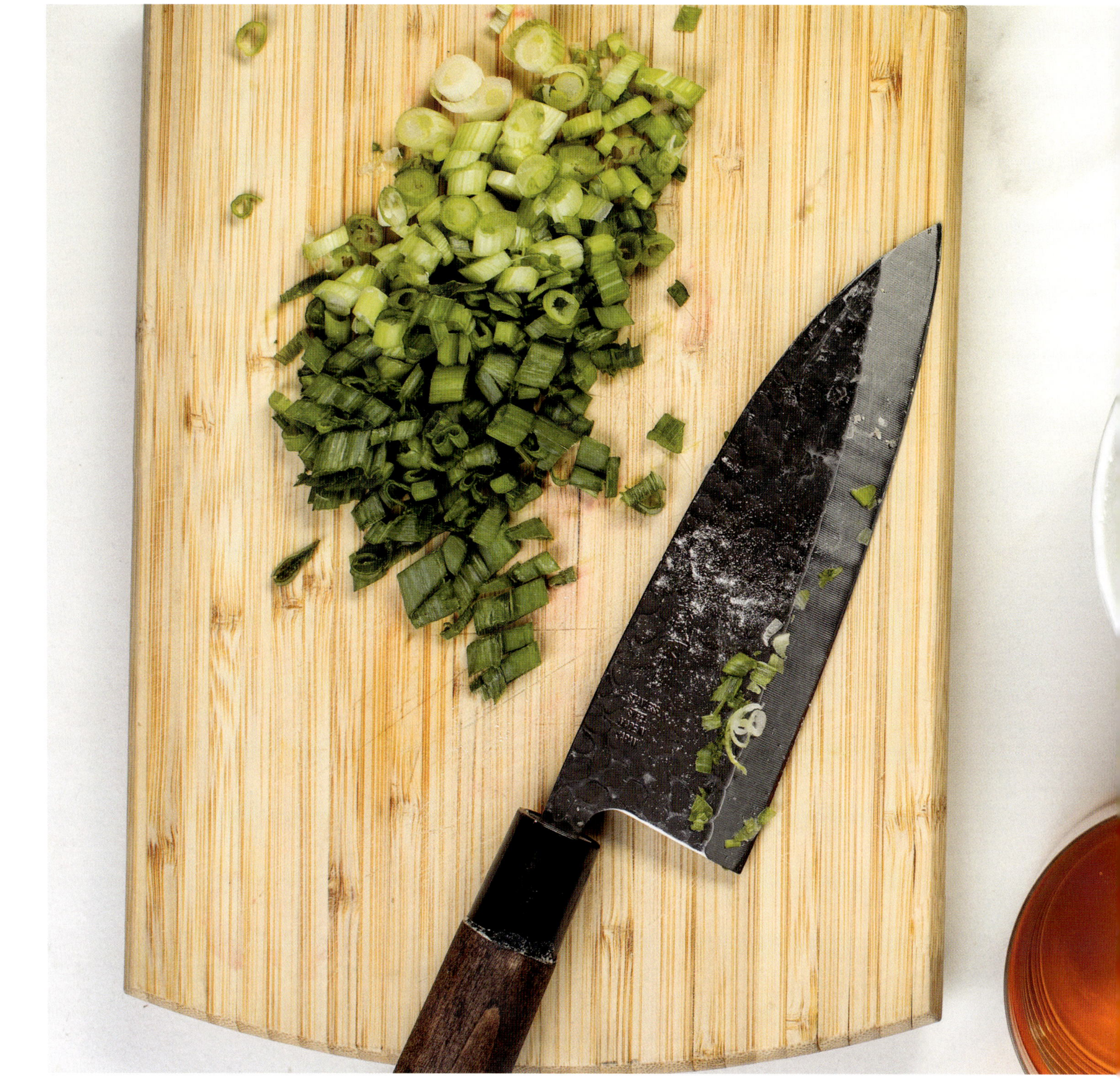

Rise & Shine

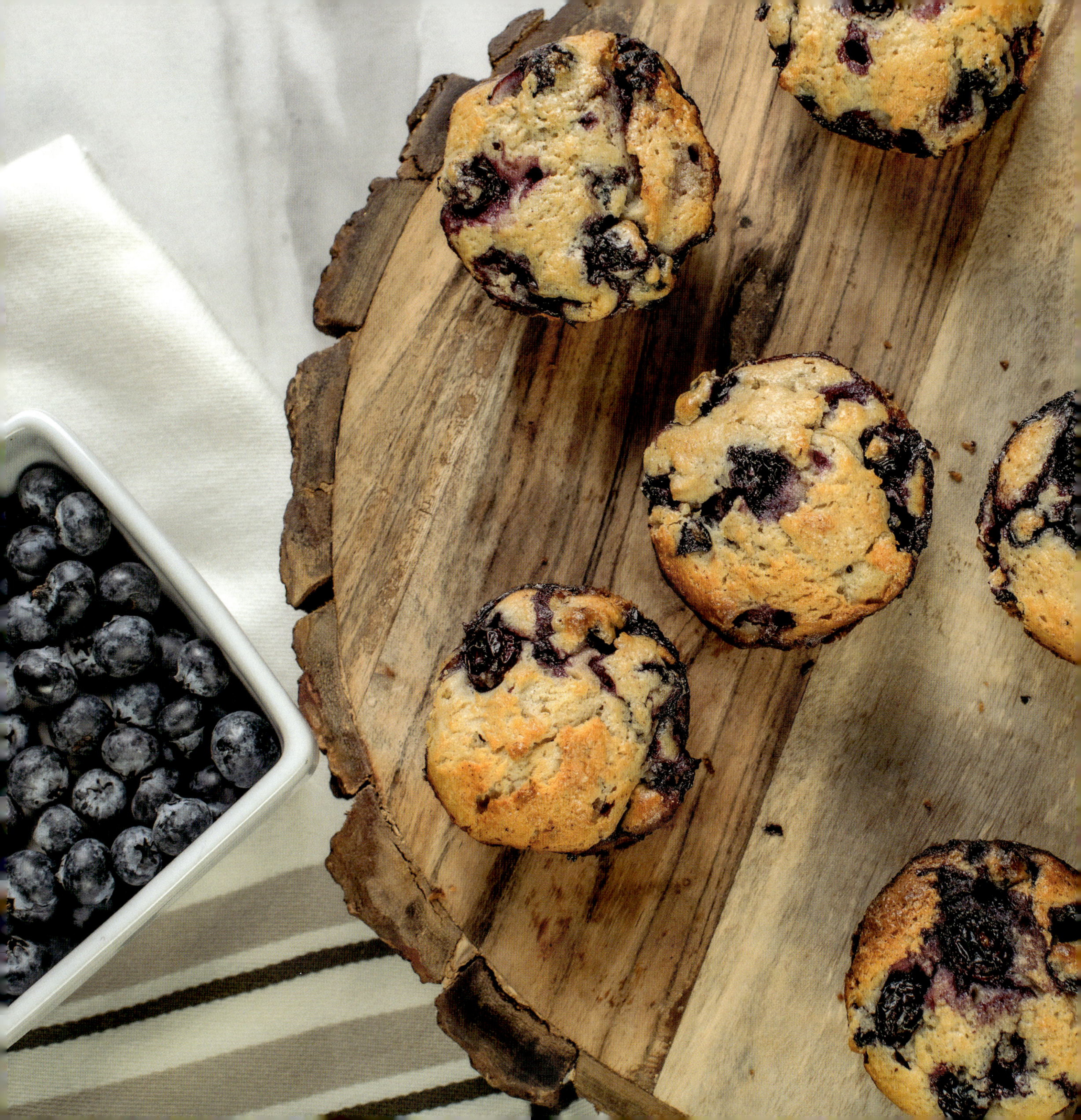

We love breakfast

Whether it happens before the sun is up or blends into brunch territory, breakfast is a whenever meal. We love greeting the sunrise standing over a stove, then sitting down for a healthy bite, packed with flavor and fuel for the day. Mornings are always better with a delicious jump start.

Breakfast Recipes

- Blueberry Muffins
- Coconut Almond Protein Balls
- Vegan Chocolate Chip Banana Bread
- Chia Pudding
- Fancy Scrambled Eggs with Truffles

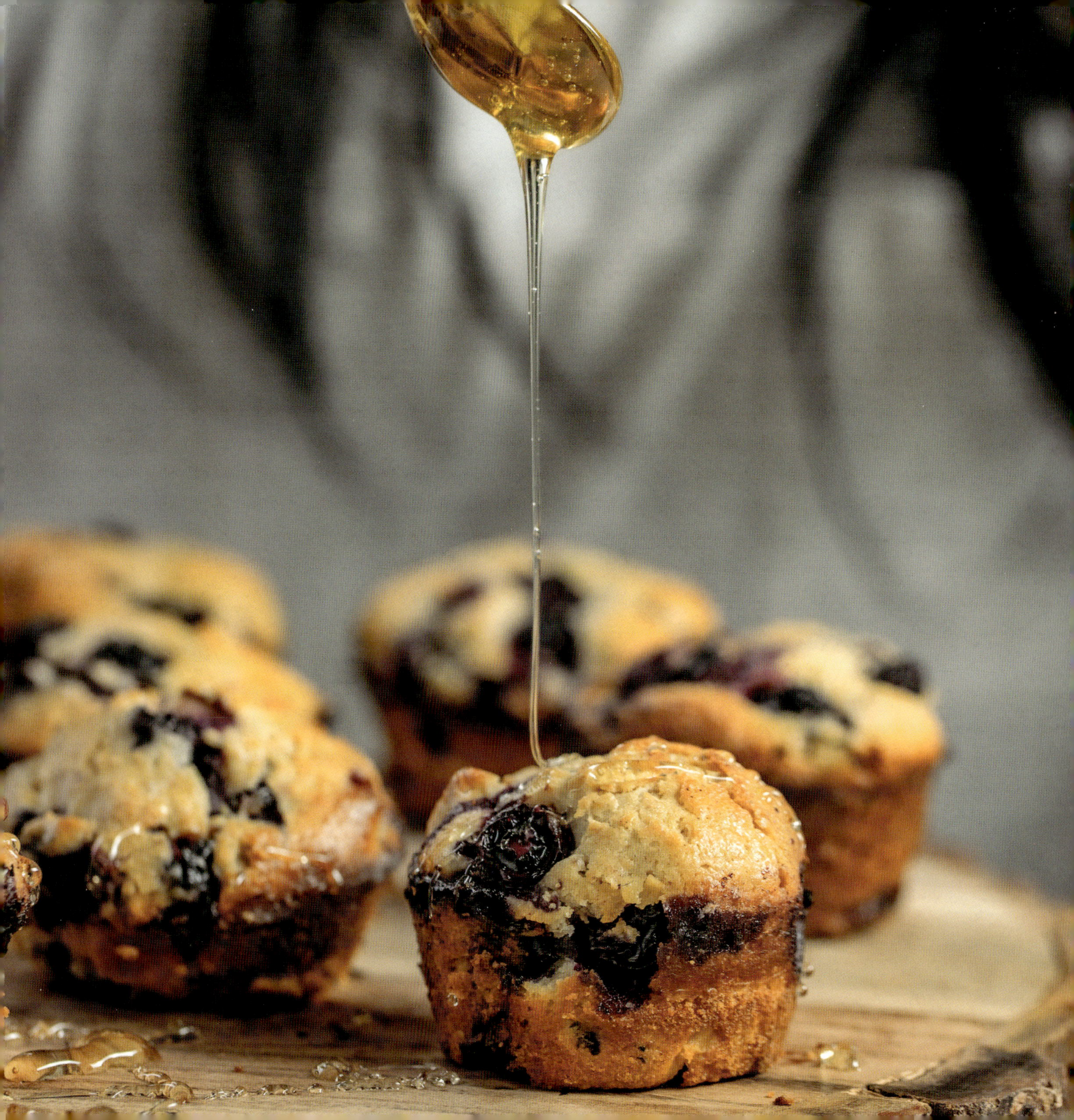

We love breakfast

Whether it happens before the sun is up or blends into brunch territory, breakfast is a whenever meal. We love greeting the sunrise standing over a stove, then sitting down for a healthy bite, packed with flavor and fuel for the day. Mornings are always better with a delicious jump start.

Breakfast Recipes

- Blueberry Muffins
- Coconut Almond Protein Balls
- Vegan Chocolate Chip Banana Bread
- Chia Pudding
- Fancy Scrambled Eggs with Truffles

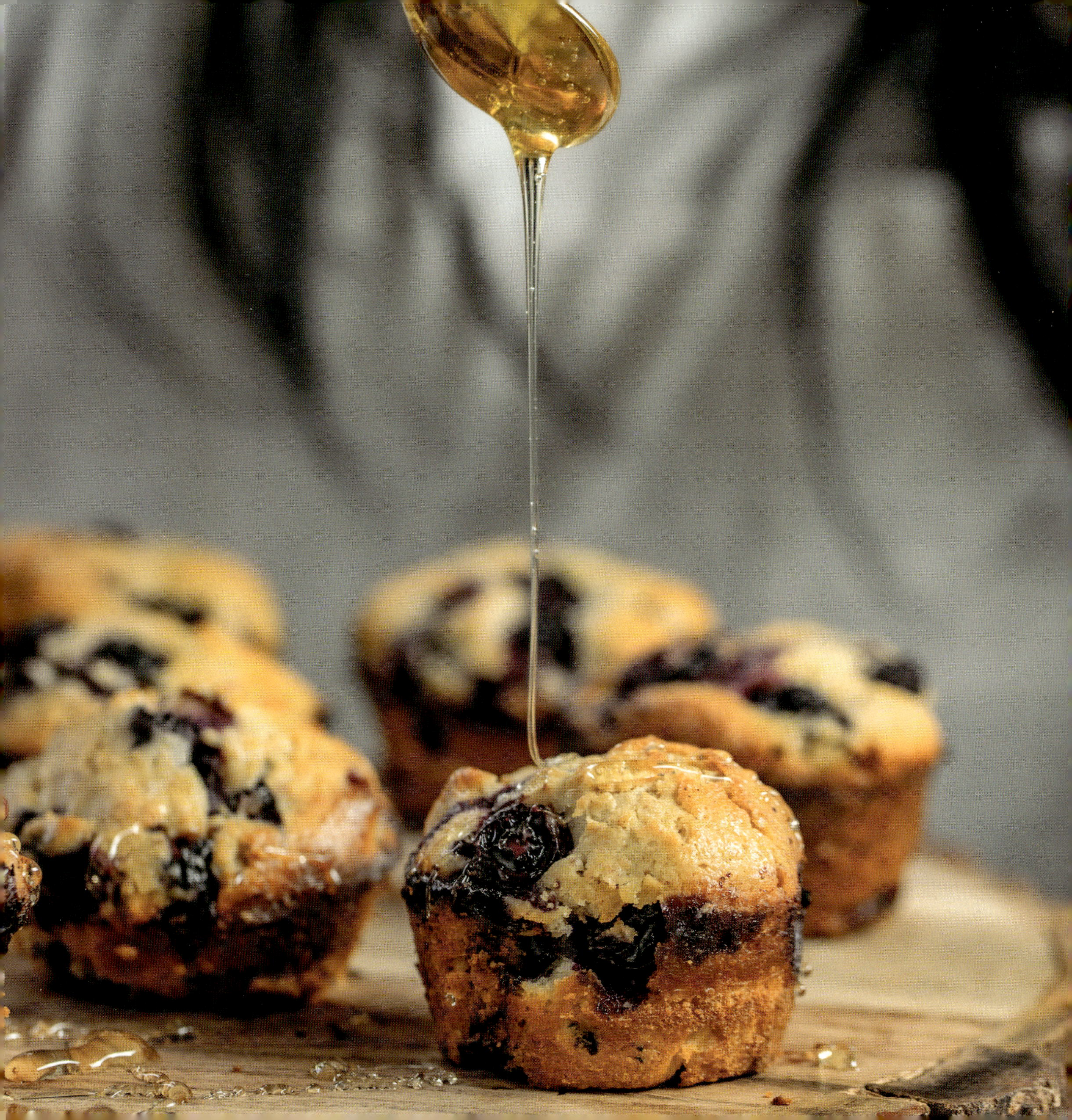

Blueberry Muffins

Prep 10 minutes

Cook 24 minutes

Serves 12 muffins

The simple joy of a muffin can't be overstated. Not only do you get to lick the spoon while you're mixing and baking, you're also readying your week for a grab-and-go mini-meal that reminds you of all the good reasons to get out of bed in the morning.

Ingredients

1 ½ cups all purpose flour
1 cup whole wheat flour
1 cup sugar or 24 packets Stevia
2 ½ tsp baking powder
½ tsp cinnamon
2 tsp kosher salt
2 cups blueberries
2 eggs + 2 egg yolks
½ cup whole milk
1 ½ cups plain yogurt
½ cup unsalted infused butter
2 tsp bourbon-based vanilla extract
1 tsp finely grated lemon zest

Preparation

Preheat the oven to 425° F. Wipe a 12-cup muffin tin with vegetable oil or nonstick spray.

Whisk together all of the dry ingredients, then add a little more than half of the blueberries and gently mix with your hands. Beat the eggs and yolks together in another bowl and set aside. In a third bowl, whisk together the remaining wet ingredients, then fold the eggs in gently, without over-stirring. Finally mix the wet and dry ingredients together along with the lemon zest.

Spoon the batter into the muffin tin, then press the remaining blueberries into the muffin tops. Sprinkle with a bit of sugar or stevia before baking for 12 minutes, rotate the muffin tin in the oven, for even coverage then bake another 12 minutes, or until a toothpick inserted into one of the muffins comes out clean.

Remove from the oven and let cool for 5 minutes in the tin before popping the muffins onto a wire rack and letting them cool completely. Spread with extra infused butter and enjoy!

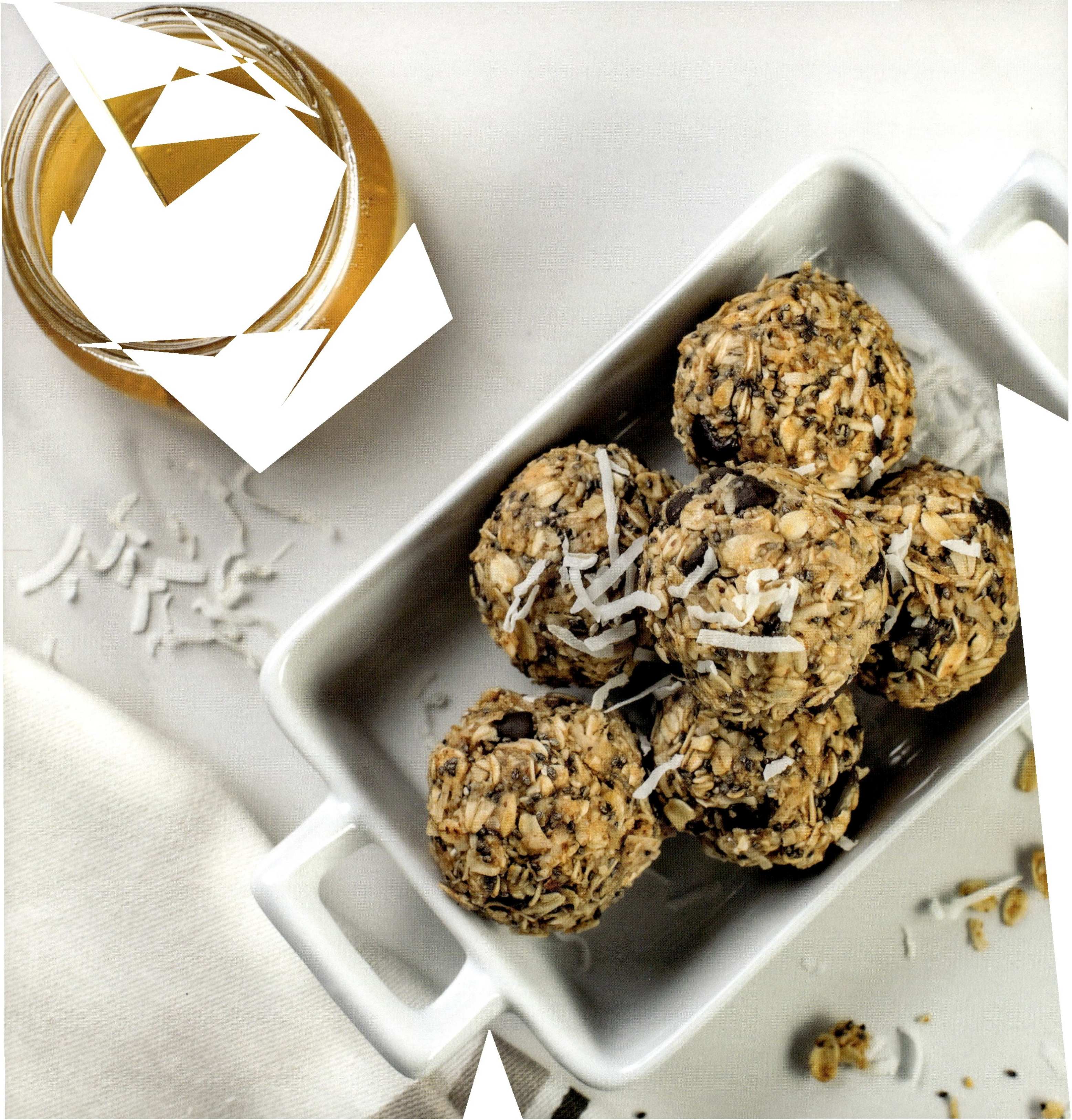

Coconut Almond Protein Balls

- **Prep** 15 minutes
- **Freeze** 15 minutes
- **Serves** 20 balls

Looking for a protein boost? Coconut and almonds aren't just for candy bars. (Although if you prefer an Almond Joy for breakfast, we're not ones to judge). Coconuts are good for your bones and metabolizing carbs, proteins, and cholesterol; almonds are some of the healthiest fats around and provide fiber, protein, and vitamin E. Plus, these nuggets of health just taste so darn good.

Ingredients

2 cups rolled oats

1 cup unsweetened shredded coconut

½ cup semi-sweet chocolate chips or cacao nips (a lower-sugar option)

¼ cup chia seeds

½ cup infused coconut oil

¼ cup infused honey; local honey is best for building up immunity to local allergies

¾ cup crunchy almond butter

1 tsp bourbon-based vanilla extract

Preparation

Mix all of the dry ingredients together. Slowly fold in the coconut oil, making sure the oil is evenly distributed. Drizzle the honey, vanilla, and almond butter, breaking up chunks with a spoon. Stir until well blended.

Put the bowl the freezer for 15 minutes, then remove and roll into golf-ball size rounds, squeezing firmly as you go.

Place in an airtight container and store in the fridge. Will keep for up to 7 days.

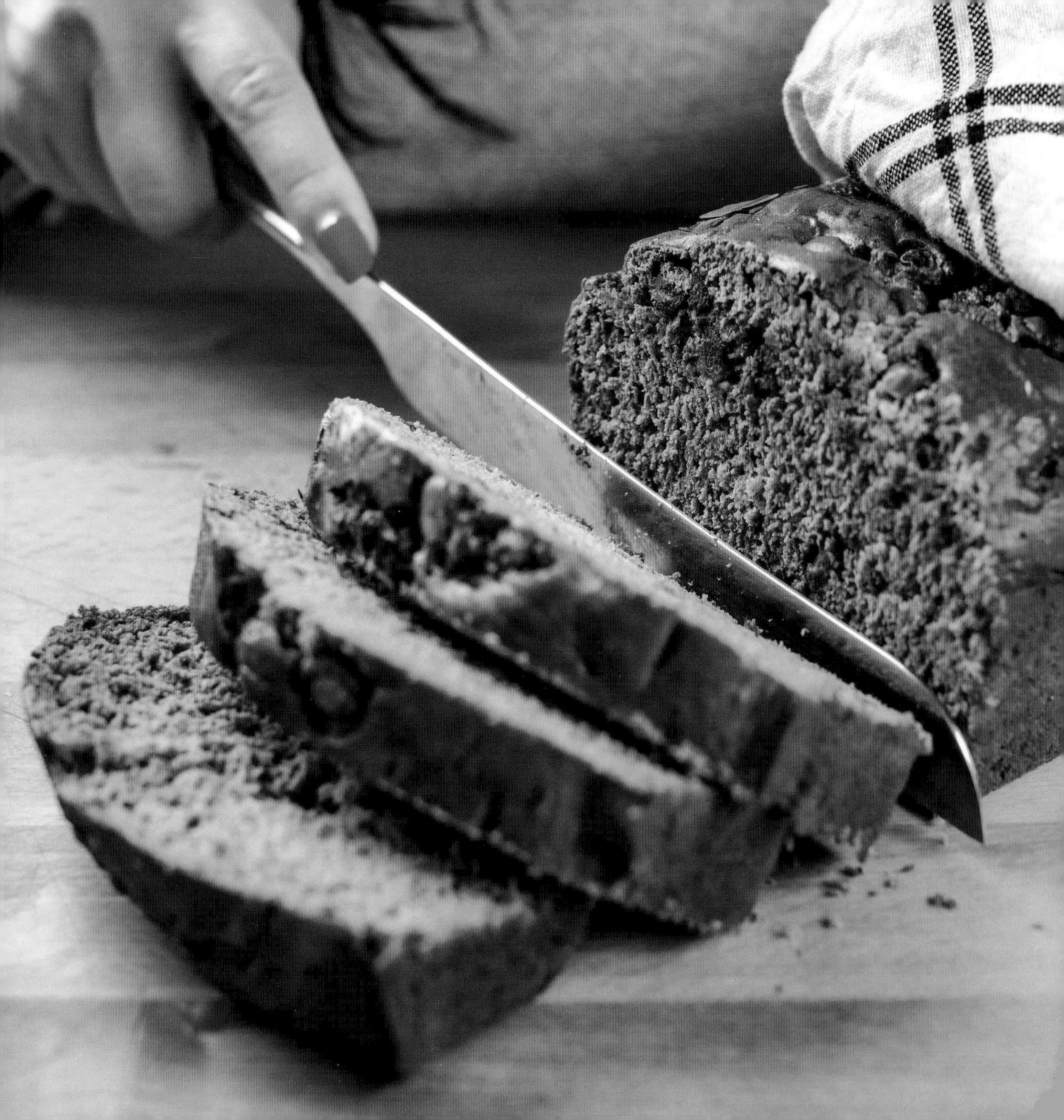

Vegan Chocolate Chip Banana Bread

A banana bread with coconut oil, plus naturally vegan dark chocolate, makes for an easily portioned breakfast (or anytime snack). The fun twist of roasting bananas intensifies their flavor and fills your house with a lovely, sweet smell. Note that we use vegan egg substitute in this one (think Bob's Red Mill egg replacer powder, rather than applesauce or aquafaba) but you can use 2 large eggs instead.

Prep 30 minutes

Cook 45 minutes

Serves 6-8 slices

Ingredients

3 bananas

1 ¾ cups white whole wheat flour

½ cup brown sugar

1 tsp baking soda

1 tsp salt

1 tsp ground cinnamon

¾ cup dark chocolate chips (verify they're vegan on the packaging)

Egg replacer equivalent of 2 eggs (follow instructions on the packaging)

½ cup unsweetened almond milk

1 tsp bourbon-based vanilla extract (no imitation flavor!)

¼ cup infused coconut oil

Preparation

Preheat your oven to 350° F. Put the unpeeled bananas on a cookie sheet and roast in the oven for 15 minutes. When they're ready, they'll be dark brown.

Mix all of the dry ingredients in a medium-sized bowl. In a separate bowl, mash the peeled bananas with a fork, then add the wet ingredients and mix thoroughly. Slowly add the dry ingredients to the wet, mixing as you go, then fold in ½ cup of the dark chocolate chips.

Pour the batter into a silicone baking bread loaf pan (or metal bread loaf pan lightly coated with nonstick cooking spray). Sprinkle the rest of the chocolate chips on top, and bake for 45 minutes.

Let it cool for 5 minutes before removing the bread from the pan. Cool for another 5 minutes on a rack.

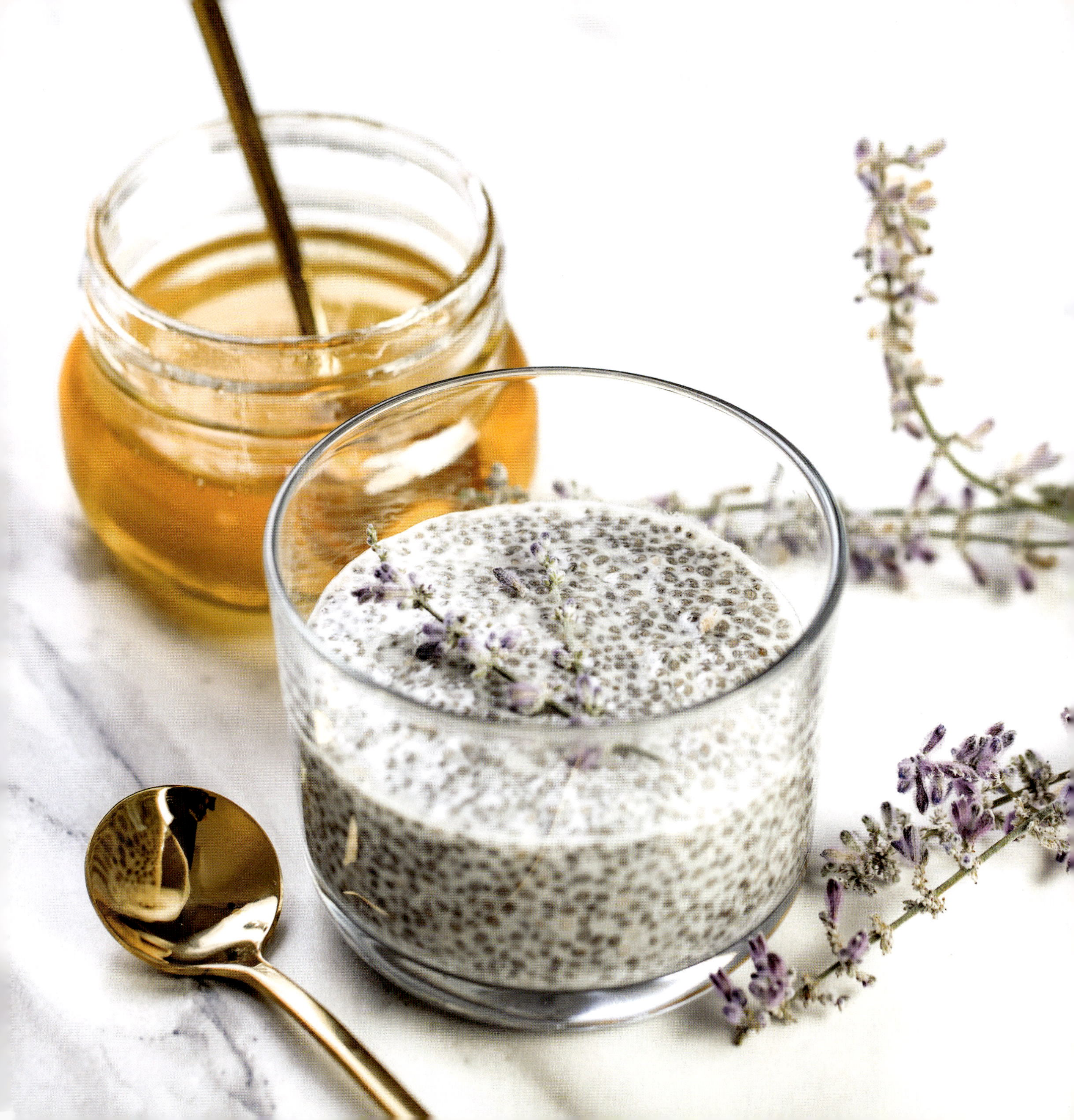

Chia Pudding

Prep 5 minutes

Chill Overnight

Serves 2 servings

Lavender and honey taste like summer by the spoonful. Combine them with chia seeds and almond milk and you've got a morning treat for your body as well as your taste buds. Make this one the night before so the chia seeds get nice and plump and pop in your mouth. And if possible, use local honey; it's a great way to build immunities to local allergies, because bees draw from the pollen in the area where you live.

Ingredients

1 cup unsweetened, unflavored almond milk

1 tsp fresh lavender buds, rinsed and dried

1 tsp bourbon-based vanilla extract

1 tsp flaky sea salt or finely ground Hawaiian pink salt

5 Tbsp chia seeds

3 Tbsp infused local honey

Preparation

Heat the milk in a sauce pan to just below the boiling point, taking it off the burner just as bubbles form at the edges. Add the lavender buds and let it rest for 10 minutes. Then strain out the buds using a sieve or coffee filter.

Mix in the salt and vanilla extract. Evenly distribute the chia seeds into 2 serving cups.

Pour the liquid over the seeds and then add the infused honey. Whisk each cup every 2 minutes for 10 minutes.

Chill in the fridge for at least 2 hours. Will keep for 4-5 days.

1 Add 2 tbsp butter to a skillet on low to medium heat. Wait until the infused butter is foaming before cracking in your eggs.

2 Stir with a fork, folding it over from the bottom of the pan. When they're thick but soft, add the cream and 1 tbsp infused butter.

3 Thinly shave black truffles over the top.

4 Season with salt and pepper.

Fancy Scrambled Eggs with Truffles

There's nobody like Jacques Pépin, the French-born American chef and author who made PBS cooking cool before TV chefs were celebrities. Among many tips and tricks he taught us is how to scramble eggs that are perfect every time. If you're looking for a delightful way to spend a Sunday morning while you're cooking, look up old episodes of his cooking shows with the equally charming Julia Child: two giants in the kitchen, understated, practical, and oh-so-good.

Prep 5 minutes

Cook 10 minutes

Serves 2-3 servings

Ingredients

6 large eggs

3 Tbsp unsalted infused butter

2 Tbsp heavy cream

Freshly ground salt and black pepper, to taste

Whole black truffle for shaving

Preparation

Crack the eggs into a bowl and beat lightly with a fork.

Heat the infused butter in a skillet over low-medium heat, swirling so the bottom and sides are completely coated.

When the butter foams, pour the eggs in and stir them slowly with a whisk or fork, keeping the eggs from sticking. When they're thick but soft, add the cream and more infused butter.

Spoon onto a plate and shave black truffles over the top to taste. Season with salt and pepper.

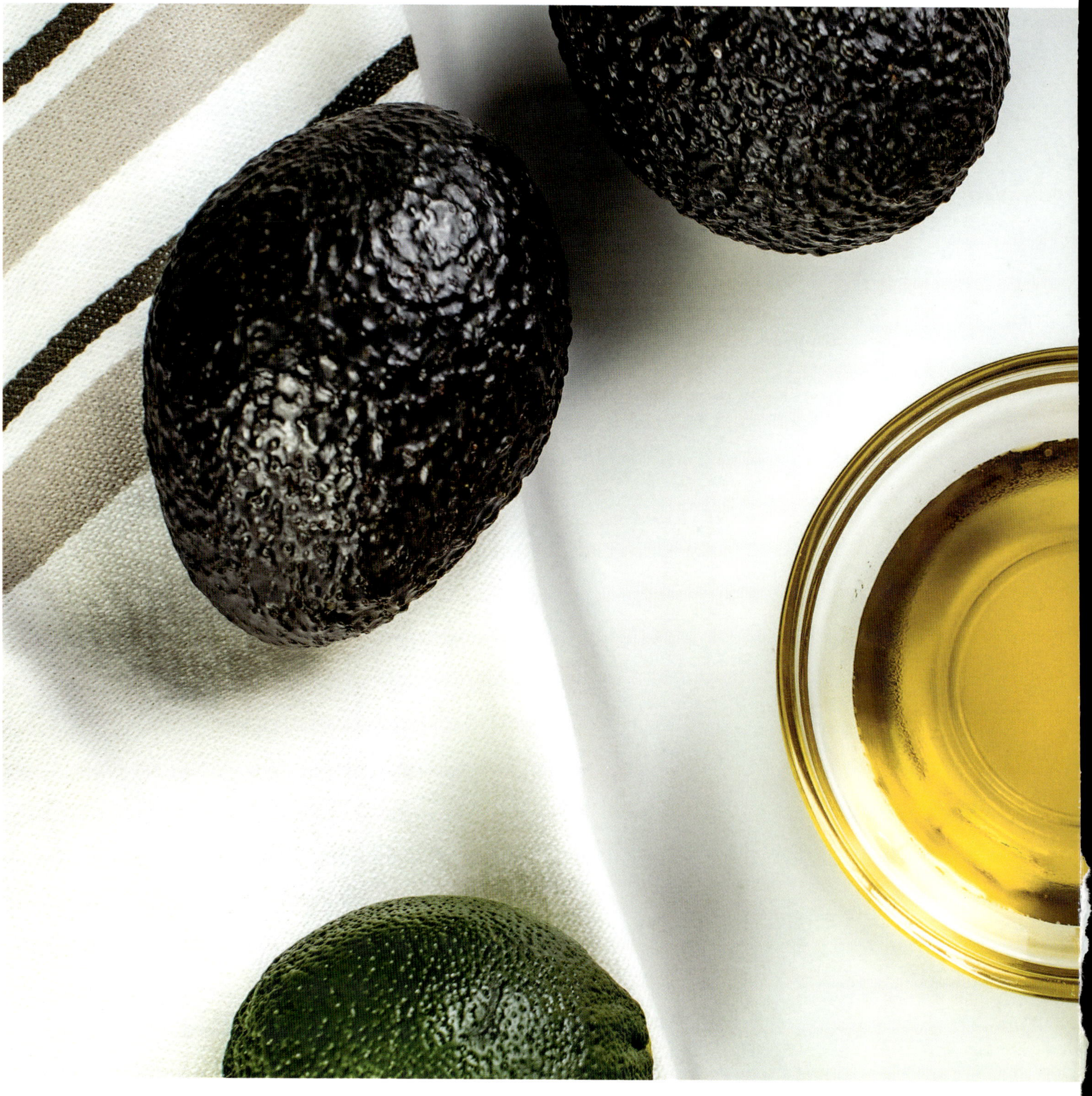

Let's Get This Party Starters

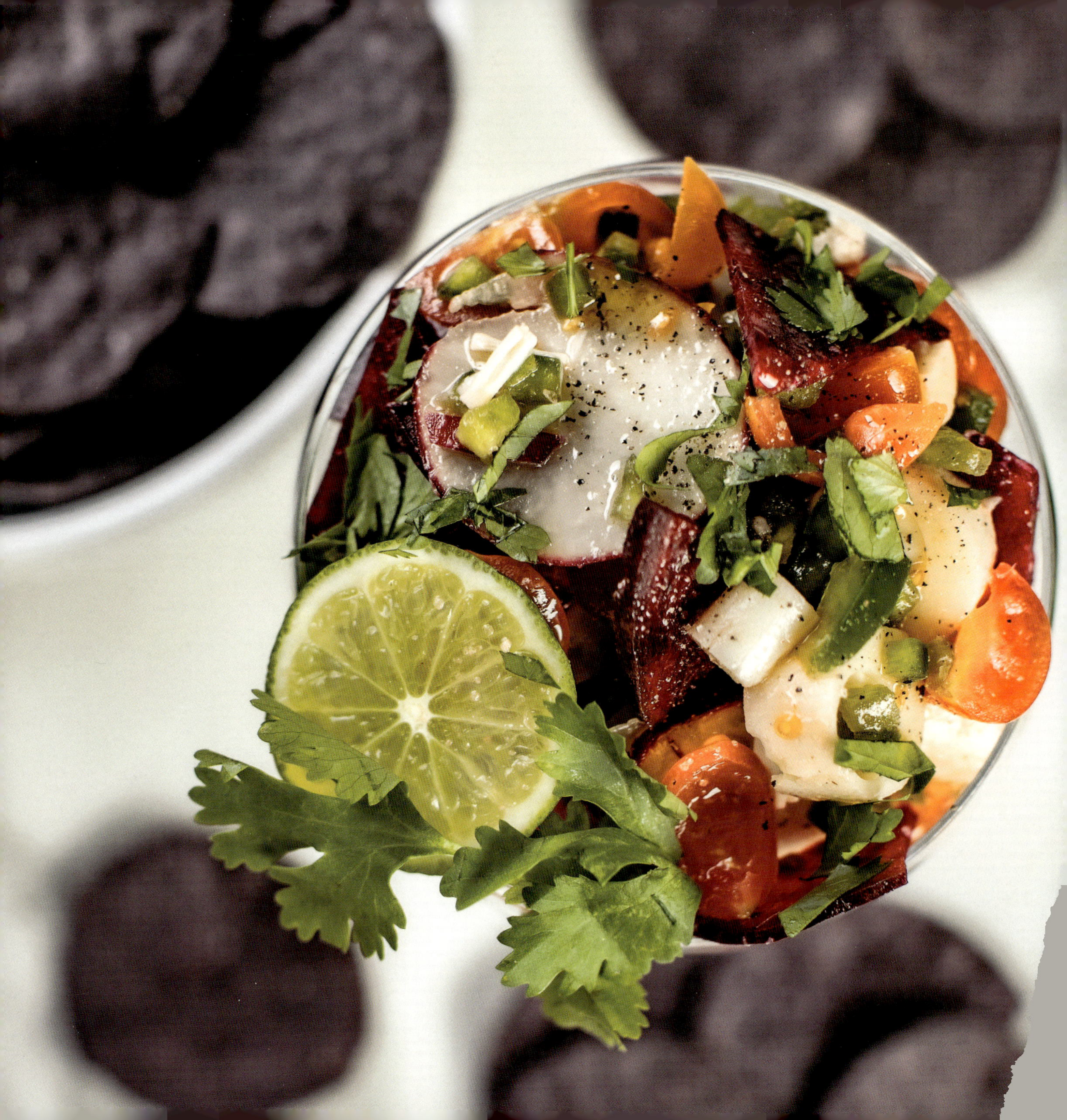

Sometimes a starter is enough

No matter the occasion, there's an app(etizer) for that. And heck, while we're at it, we're giving options that can double as side dishes — from a Korean scallion pancake to Orzo pasta that makes the meal. Whether you're looking for a great app or a side dish, we've got you covered.

Starters Recipes

- Guac
- Vegan Ceviche
- Hasselback Potato
- Creamy Lemon Zucchini Orzo
- Garlic Cauli-Bites
- Pajeon (Korean Scallion Pancake)

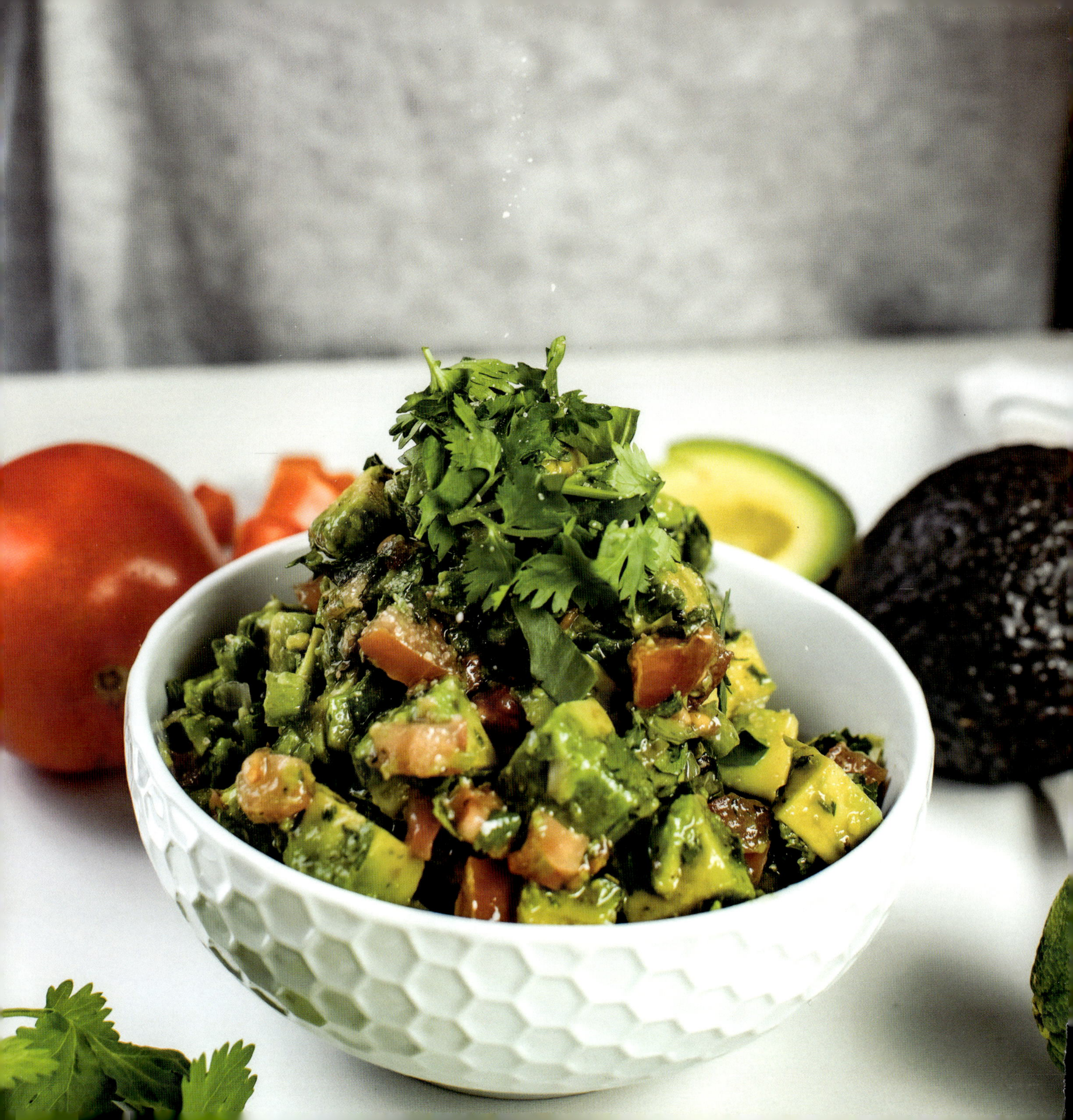

Guac

Prep 10 minutes

Serves 4-5 servings

We like our guacamole chunky, rather than super-mashed or puréed. However you take yours, it's hard to argue with all of that vegan, dairy-free, gluten-free, healthy, fatty goodness.

Ingredients

3 medium ripe Haas avocados, cut into ¼ inch chunks

1 green chile, seeded and minced

2 spring onions or white onion, thinly sliced

½ cup roughly chopped cilantro

1 Roma tomato, diced

2-3 tsp infused coconut oil

Juice of 1 lime

Freshly ground salt and black pepper

Preparation

Stir together the avocado, chile, onion, cilantro and tomato in a medium-sized bowl.

Drizzle with lime juice and infused coconut oil and season with salt and pepper to taste.

Grab your favorite chips or veggie slices and dive in.

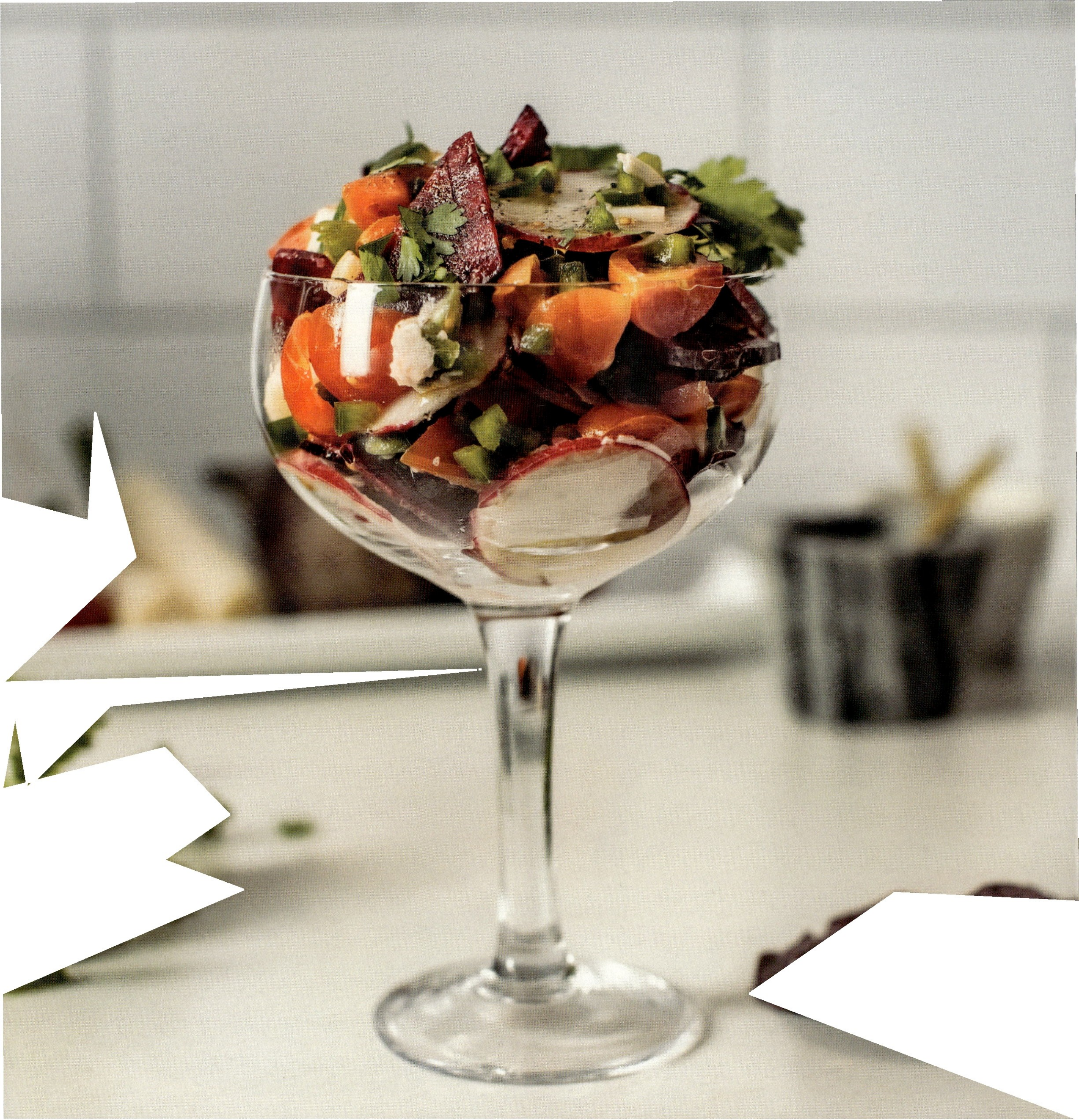

Vegan Ceviche

Soak Overnight
Prep 20 minutes

Serves 3-4 servings

Seafood ceviche lovers rise up! And by rise up, we mean open up your minds to this lovely, light, and flavorful dish that was inspired by our vegan fans. The secret? Hearts of palm.

Ingredients

7 hearts of palm, sliced
2 sheets of Kombu seaweed
¼ cup lime juice
¼ cup orange juice
¼ cup infused olive oil
1 Tbsp minced jalapeño
1 Tbsp minced red chili
¼ cup blood orange segments, roughly chopped
4 radishes, preferably a peppery variety like Mirabeau, sliced
4 beets, sliced
8 cherry tomatoes
1 sprig of cilantro, chopped
Salt and pepper to taste

Preparation

Soak the sliced hearts of palm in a bowl of water overnight with 2 sheets of Kombu seaweed, to soften them, or use canned hearts of palm and soak for two hours.

The next day, drain the water out of the bowl and remove the Kombu, then add the juices, infused olive oil, jalapeño, chili, and light salt to the hearts of palm. Marinate for 30 minutes.

Add the remaining ingredients, cover and refrigerate for 30 more minutes. Serve chilled.

1 Place two chopsticks under your potato to keep from cutting all of the way through.

2 Insert herbs of your choice in the slits. We love garlic, rosemary, and thyme!

3 Be sure to baste with infused oil regularly while baking.

4 One final douse of oil, along with salt and pepper, and you're ready to dive in.

Hasselback Potato

- **Prep** 10 minutes
- **Cook** 40 minutes
- **Serves** 1 serving

The humble potato, upgraded courtesy of Swedish chefs. No, not the Muppets' Swedish Chef — although we're sure that he could have rocked this dish. A Hasselback potato is remarkably easy to make, smells wonderful as it bakes, and tastes like a million bucks. We drizzle flower-infused olive oil after it's done baking so the potency stays intact.

Ingredients

1 large Russet potato
2 Tbsp fresh rosemary
2 Tbsp fresh thyme
3 cloves garlic
4 Tbsp regular olive oil
1 Tbsp infused olive oil
Salt and black pepper

Preparation

Preheat your oven to 425° F. Wash the potato and place it on a cutting board.

Using a very sharp knife, cut the potato crosswise into slices around 1/8 of an inch thick, being careful to cut as far as possible without slicing all of the way through — so the entire potato is still intact at the base. Slice the garlic and place a single slice in each slit, along with rosemary and thyme.

In an oven-proof dish, drizzle with regular olive oil and bake for 40 minutes or until the potato leaves are crisp, basting with the oil from the pan every 10 minutes.

When done, drizzle the infused oil over the top. Season to taste with salt and pepper.

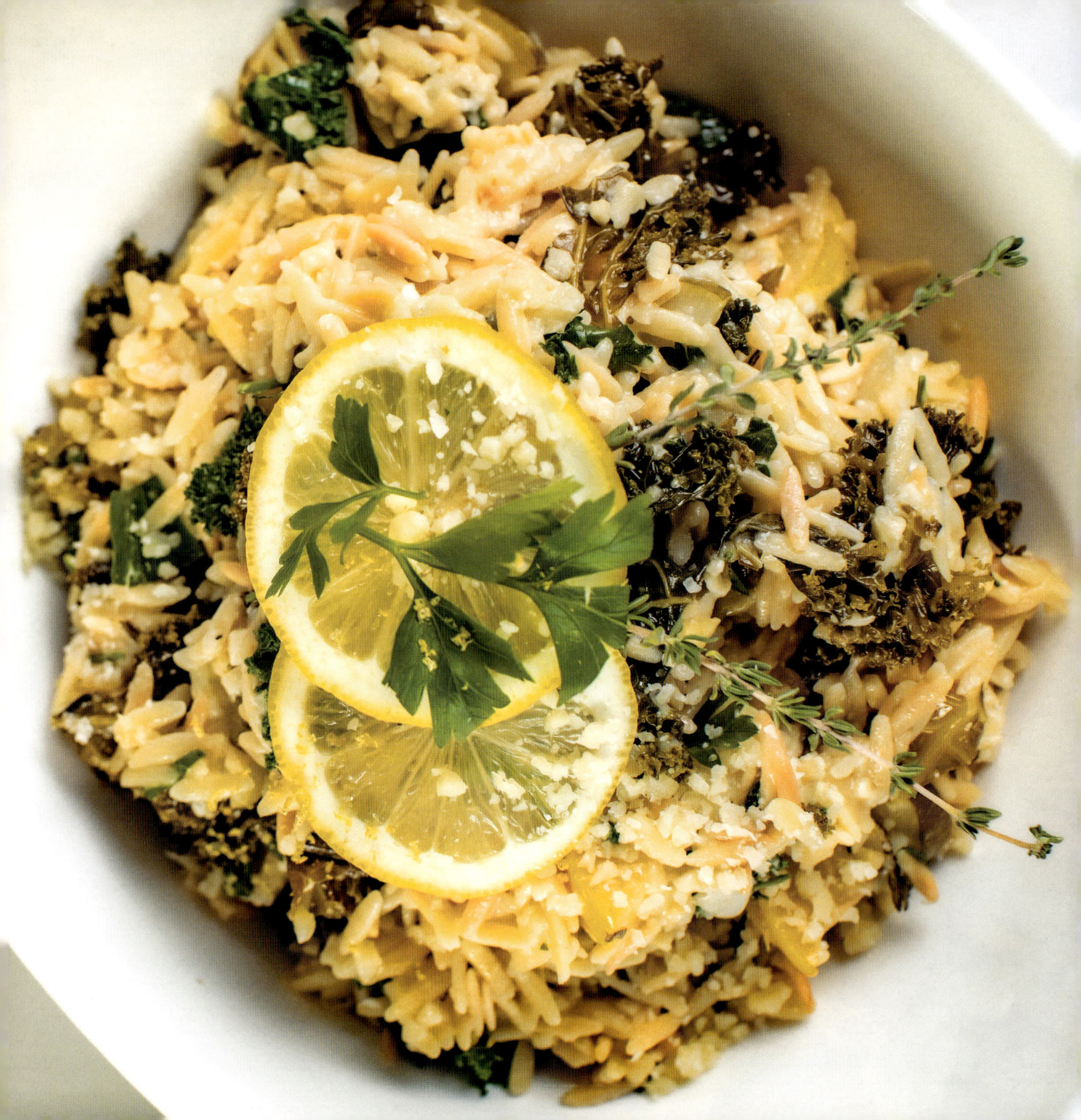

Creamy Lemon Zucchini Orzo

This recipe, inspired by the folks at Half Baked Harvest, had us at "Creamy Lemon Cheese." And the dish lives up to its name — the slight bitterness of the zucchini and soft, pillowy orzo never tasted so good. We're adding flower-infused butter at the end because boiling it for too long can affect potency.

Prep 15 minutes

Cook 20 minutes

Serves 2-4 servings

Ingredients

3 Tbsp regular butter

2 Tbsp infused butter

3-4 cloves garlic, minced or grated

1 pound dry orzo pasta (or gluten-free orzo pasta)

2 Tbsp fresh thyme leaves

2 medium zucchini and or yellow summer squash, grated

1/2 bunch kale, finely shredded

3 cups low sodium chicken or vegetable broth

Zest and juice of 1 lemon

1 tsp onion powder

Freshly ground salt and black pepper

1/2 cup canned full fat coconut milk

2 Tbsp chopped fresh parsley

3/4 cup grated Parmesan cheese

Preparation

Melt regular butter in a big skillet over medium-high heat, then cook the garlic for 1 minute.

Stir in orzo and thyme. After 2-3 minutes, add in vegetables. When kale is wilted, add the broth. Scrape crispy bits off the bottom of the pan and stir.

Add lemon juice and onion powder. Season with salt and pepper to taste.

Turn heat to high. Once it begins to boil, lower the heat to low and simmer for 10 minutes.

Stir in the coconut milk, infused butter, and Parmesan (if using), adding more broth if necessary to bring it to a creamy consistency until the pasta is cooked.

Top with more Parmesan or nutritional yeast and parsley.

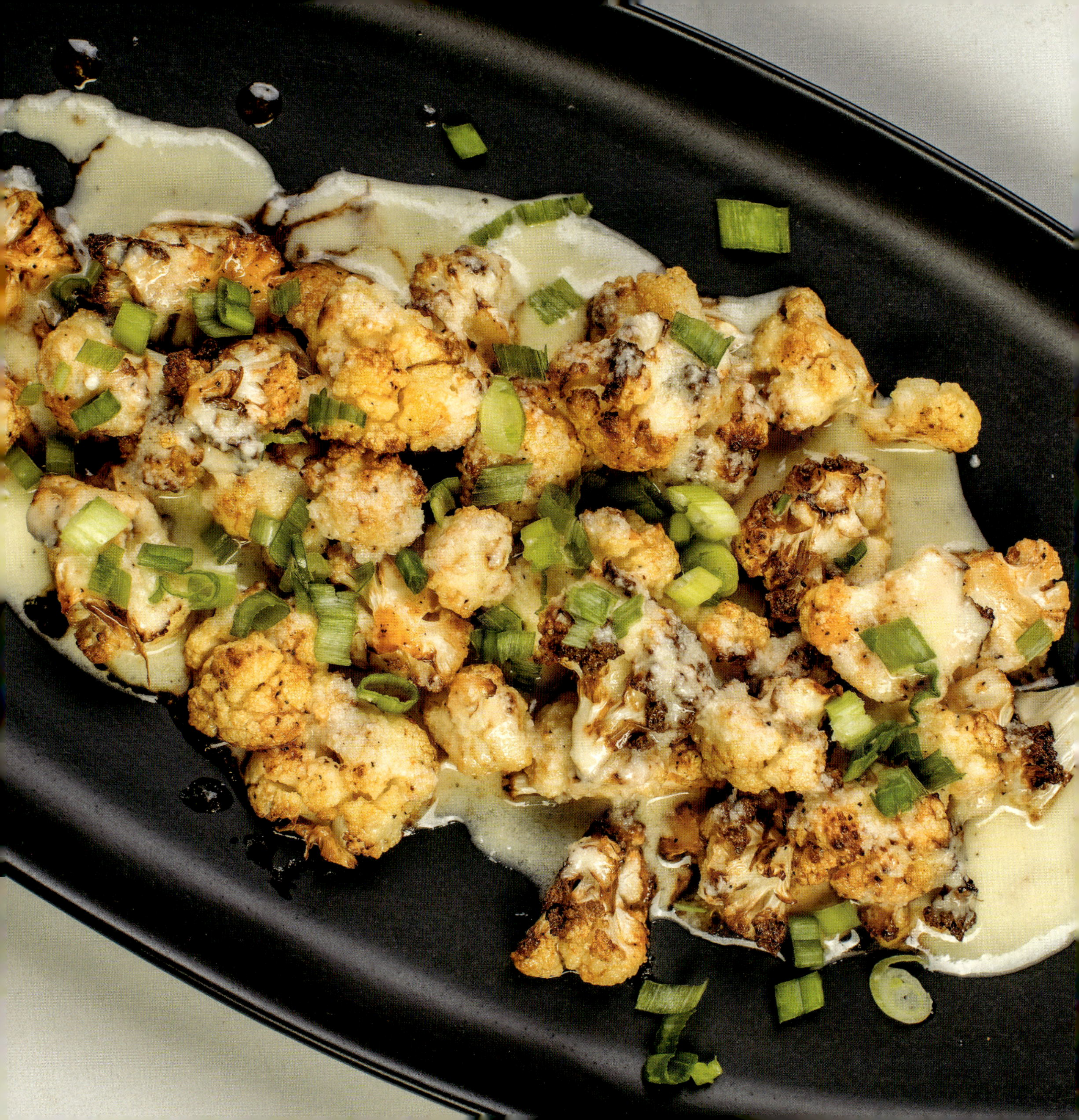

Garlicky Cauli-Bites

Prep 15 minutes

Cook 25 minutes

Serves 4 servings

Cauliflower is having a moment in the sun. It's everywhere: in pizza crusts, vegan fried chicken spin-offs, smoothies, even cocktails. Cauli-recipes offer a reduction in calories and an uptick in fiber and vitamins. Our version includes a vegan Lebanese garlic sauce called Toum.

Ingredients

1 head cauliflower, cut into florets
2 Tbsp olive oil
1 tsp hot sauce of your choice
¼ tsp cayenne pepper
Freshly ground salt and pepper

For the Toum garlic sauce:

8 garlic cloves
2 Tbsp lemon juice
1 tsp sea salt
½ cups regular coconut oil
2 Tbsp infused coconut oil
2 Tbsp ice water

Preparation

Preheat your oven to 425° F.

Toss all of the non-Toum ingredients in a bowl and spread on a baking sheet. Roast for 15 minutes. Give the sheet a gentle but firm shake, then roast for another 10 minutes, until the cauliflower has turned golden.

While it's roasting, prepare the Toum. Pop the garlic into a food processor and mince by pulsing the processor and scraping the sides down with a rubber spatula. Add 1 Tbsp lemon juice and salt and keep pulsing until it becomes a paste. Turn the processor on low and pour in the melted, infused coconut oil. Then pour in the rest of the lemon juice, followed by ice water. Continue until the Toum is light and fluffy.

Drizzle the Toum over the bites and serve warm.

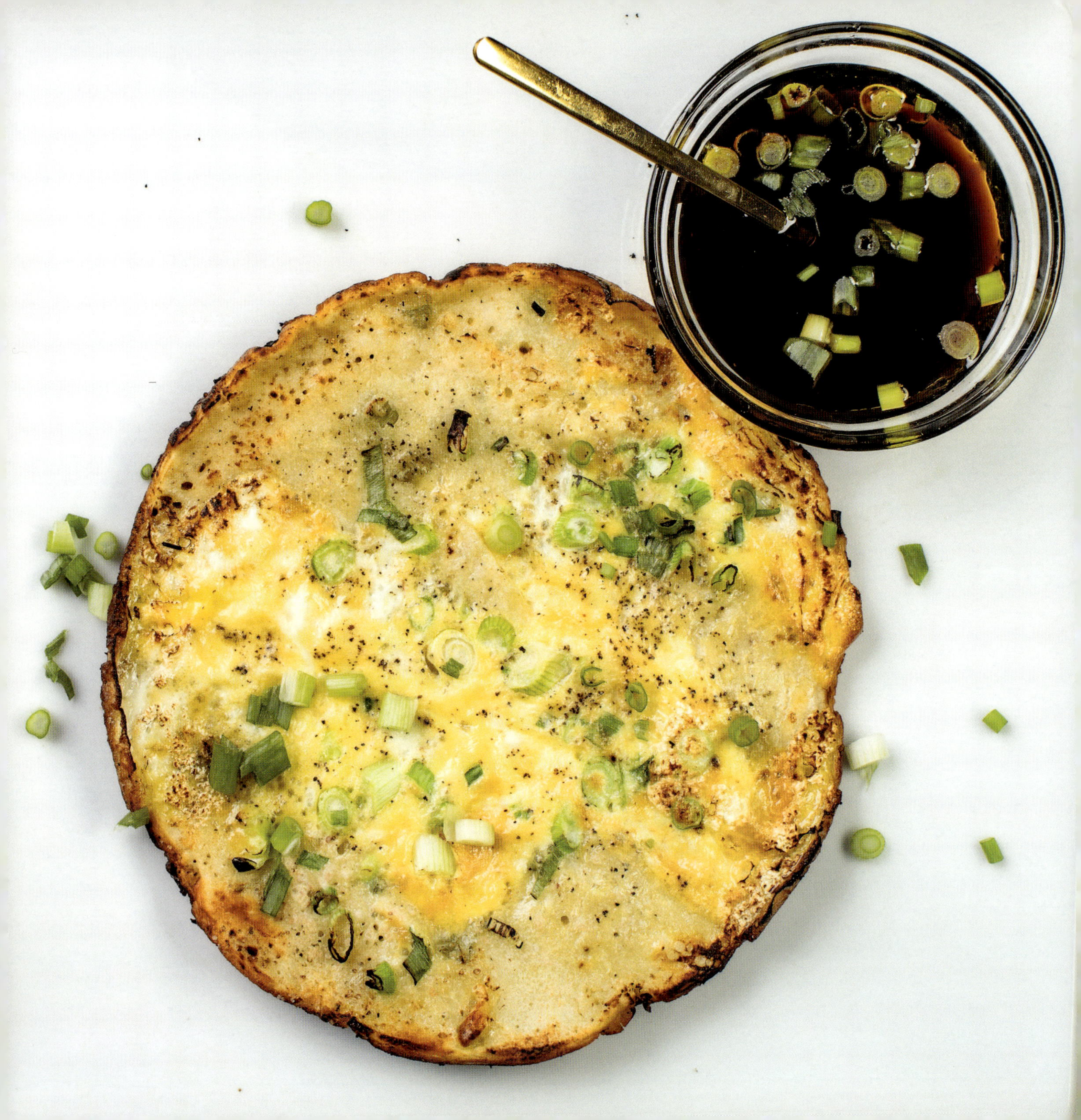

Pajeon
(Korean Scallion Pancake)

Prep 15 minutes

Cook 15 minutes

Serves 2-4 servings

Bless David Chang. The Momofuku founder, creative director, and chef is unafraid to riff on timeless ideas and preparations. Here's our infused spin-off of his Korean street pancake recipe. Get creative with the toppings! Experiment with chopping anything from veggies to pork belly on top.

Ingredients

1 cup all purpose flour
½ cup lager beer
3 Tbsp infused coconut oil, melted
3 Tbsp regular cooking oil
½ tsp salt
1 large egg, lightly beaten
1 bunch of scallions
1 Tbsp soy sauce

Top with optional ingredients, from leftover vegetables to sautéed shrimp to your favorite kimchi, but here we keep it simple and serve with a dipping sauce.

Dipping sauce ingredients:
3 Tbsp soy sauce
2 Tbsp rice vinegar
3 drops sesame oil
1 drop chile olive oil

Preparation

Pour the flour, beer, infused oil, and salt into a bowl; let the bubbles relax and then stir until just mixed. Chop the green tops of the scallions into 1 inch pieces, and set aside the whites.

Heat the regular oil in a large skillet over medium-high heat and fry the green scallions until they're soft. Add the soy sauce and toss a few times. Next, pour the batter over the scallions and cook until the bottom starts to get brown and crispy. But don't flip it yet! Pour the beaten egg over the batter and cook until the egg begins to firm near the edges.

Now it's time to flip — but if you poured the pancake too big to flip with a spatula, don't worry! Simply slide it onto a dinner plate and flip it back into the skillet. Cook until the egg is crispy.

Cool the pancake on a cutting board before cutting into wedges. Mix together dipping sauce ingredients in a small bowl. Serve pancakes with dipping sauce and toppings.

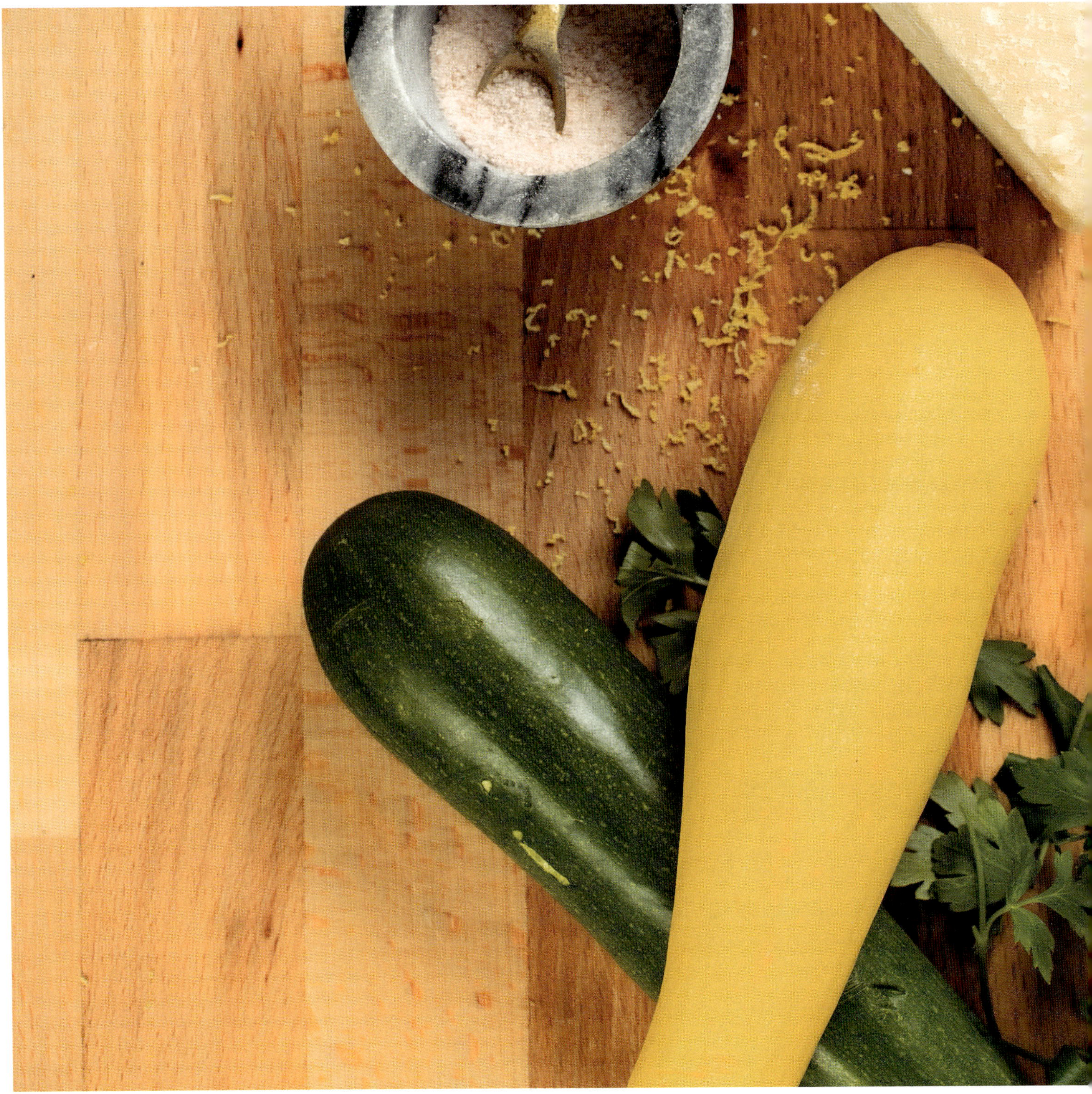

Main Strains

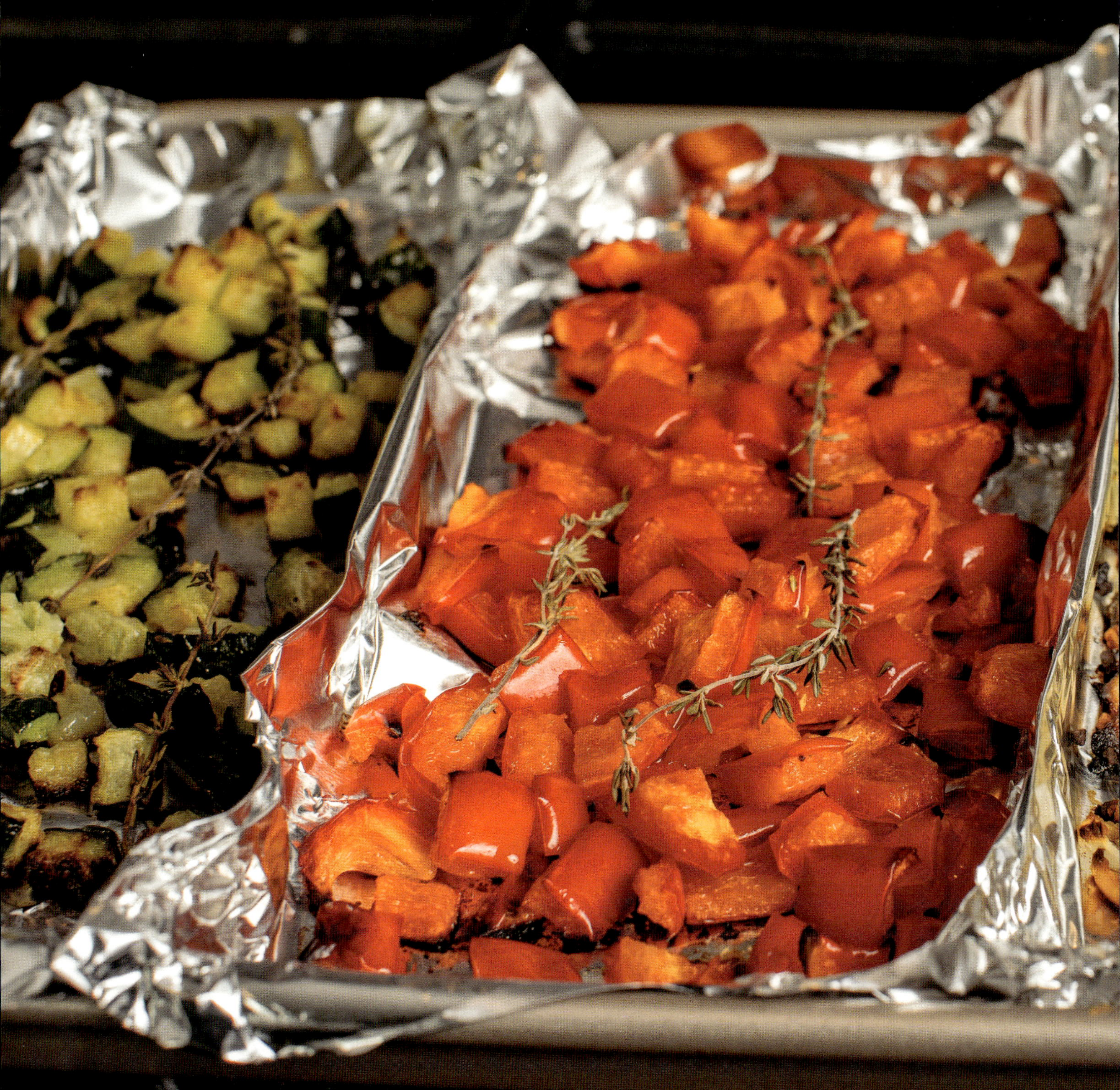

The Big Guns

These are the entrees, the main courses, and the crowd pleasers, made to share with friends, family, and Instagram followers. Get ready to be full.

Entrees Recipes

- Curried Chicken Thighs
- Watermelon Togarashi Salad
- Ratatouille
- Mac & Cheese & Veg
- The Only Roast Chicken You'll Ever Need

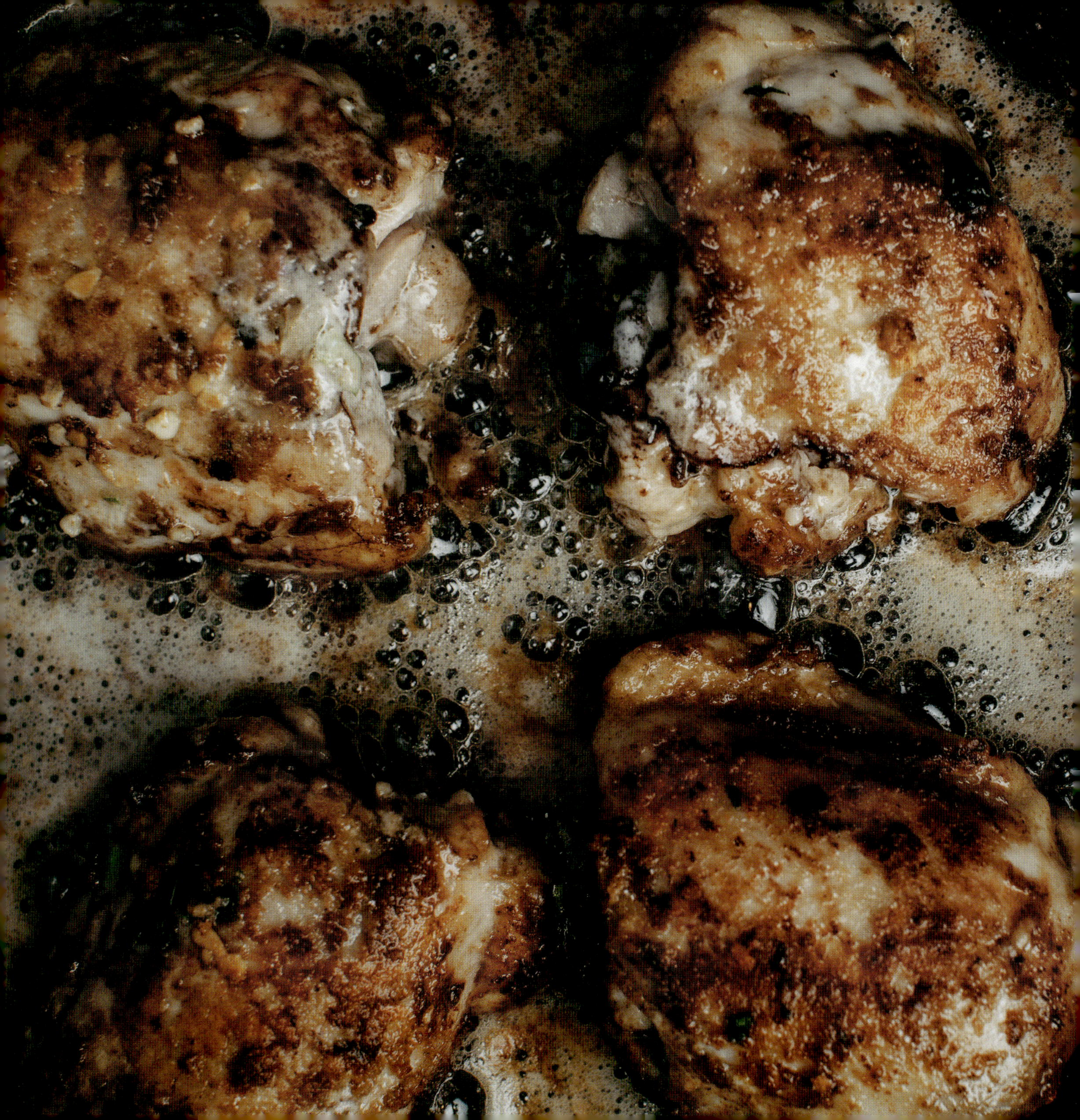

Curried Chicken Thighs

Marinate 24 hours
Prep 20 minutes

Cook 45 minutes

Serves 4 thighs

A spicy curry is perhaps the world's best hangover food. Also, its strong flavors and smells complement flower-infused oil, making it a great introductory dish for people who are just starting out with infused cooking. This curry starts with a recipe from James Beard award winning chef Asha Gomez, who draws on her Indian heritage, mixing Kerala flavors with a down south vibe.

Ingredients

4 boneless, skinless chicken thighs
1 cup buttermilk
3 Tbsp infused coconut oil
5 cloves of garlic
3 jalapeños, minced including seeds
½ cup fresh cilantro leaves & stalks
¼ cup fresh mint leaves
¾ Tbsp salt
1 cup all purpose flour
1/2 cup frying oil
¼ cup lime zest

Preparation

Put the buttermilk, oil, garlic, jalapeños, cilantro, mint, and salt into a food processor and blend.

Pour over the chicken thighs in tupperware. Cover and refrigerate for 24 hours.

Get the marinated chicken and dredge it in flour and fry over medium heat, turning every 2 minutes for 12 minutes, until golden brown. Let cool on a rack. Wipe the pan dry and return to heat, then cook the leftover marinade for 5 minutes, stirring so it won't burn.

Serve by pouring some of the marinade into each dish and placing a chicken thigh on top, then zesting the lime over.

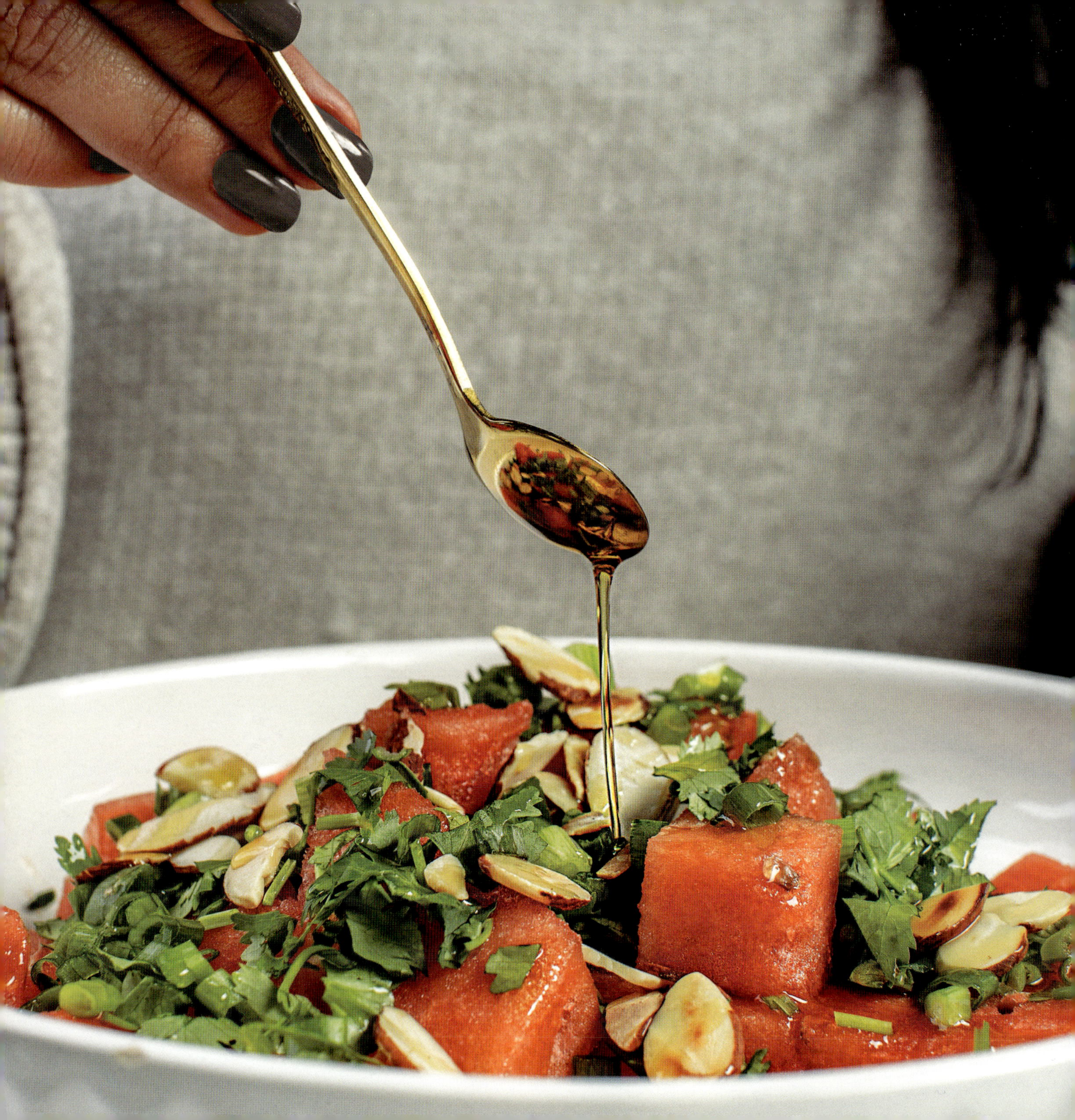

Watermelon Togarashi Salad

Dry 1 hour
Prep 15 minutes

Serves 4-6 servings

A meaty mouthful of watermelon is not only filling, but hits you with a handful of antioxidants, amino acids, and anti-inflammatories. And those are just the benefits that start with the letter A! Trust us, this one's worth filling up a plate.

Ingredients

1 Tbsp orange zest
3 tsp cayenne pepper
2 tsp sesame seeds
1 Tbsp ginger
½ sheet nori (dried seaweed)
5 cups watermelon
2 scallions
½ cup toasted almond slices
¼ cup fresh cilantro
3 Tbsp infused olive oil to drizzle

Preparation

For the Togarashi seasoning blend, use a microplane or zester to extract the orange zest and ginger. Mix them together and Dry in the LĒVO for 1 hour at 150° F. Once dried, combine with cayenne pepper and sesame seeds.

Next, take the nori seaweed and wave it over the flame of a gas burner until the corners curl and turn crisp. If you're not feeling quite so Indiana Jones, you can roast it under a broiler, flipping every couple of minutes, until it crisps. Crumble it into your spice mixture, then tip all of it into a mortar and pestle and grind until it's powder.

Cut your watermelon into bite-sized chunks. Mix with finely chopped scallions, toasted almond slices, and cilantro. Drizzle with infused olive oil, then serve immediately!

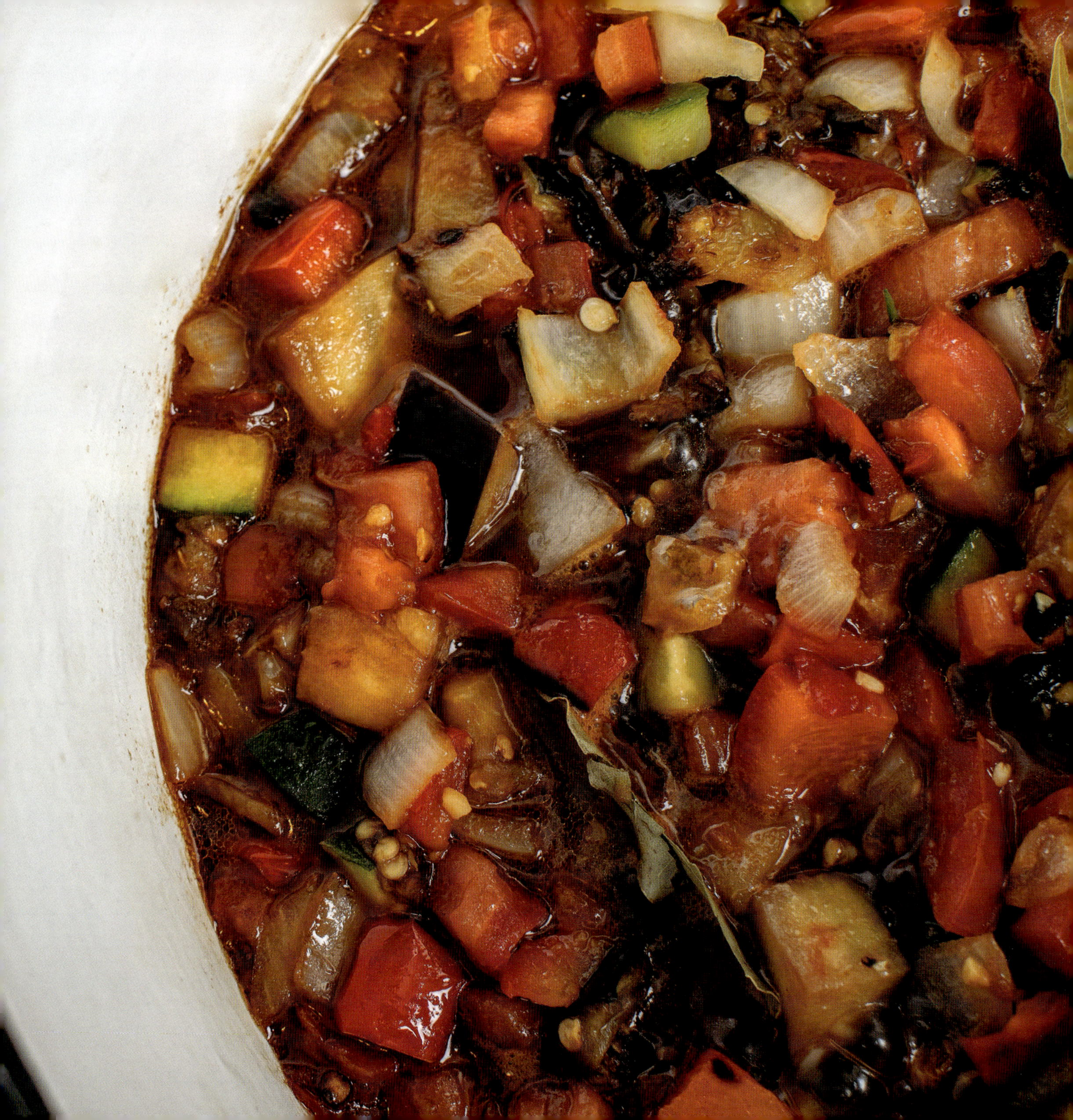

Ratatouille

Prep 20 minutes

Cook 1 hour 45 min

Serves 6-8 servings

Originally a French peasant dish, this dish has had many variations from Provençal villages to Pixar big screens, but if there's one thing we've learned, it's to cook the vegetables separately. It's a little bit more of a hassle, but it makes a big difference.

Ingredients

1 yellow onion
1 zucchini
2 red bell peppers
1 small eggplant
3 garlic cloves
6 sprigs of fresh thyme
4 Tbsp regular olive oil
3 Roma tomatoes
1 bay leaf
4-6 Tbsp of infused olive oil
Salt and black pepper

Preparation

Preheat the oven to 350° F.
Cut the onions, zucchini, and peppers into ¼ inch thick cubes, and the eggplant into ½ inch cubes.

Spread each of the vegetables onto their own baking sheet; lined with aluminum foil. Mince two garlic cloves and add to onion. Add two sprigs of thyme to pepper, zucchini, and eggplant. Salt everything lightly, then drizzle 1 Tbsp of infused olive oil onto each of the trays. Bake the onions for an hour, the eggplant for 45 minutes, and the peppers for 35 minutes — gently shaking every 15 minutes.

While they cook, bring a pot of water to a boil and blanch the tomatoes until the skins split, then drop them into ice water and peel them when cooled. Seed the tomatoes but keep the juices, then dice and let them soak in their juices. Mince the remaining clove of garlic and add it to the tomatoes, along with the bay leaves.

When the veggies are done cooking, combine them with the tomatoes in a saucepan. Cover with more infused olive oil and sprinkle again with salt. Cook on medium heat for 45 minutes. Season with salt and pepper to taste and serve.

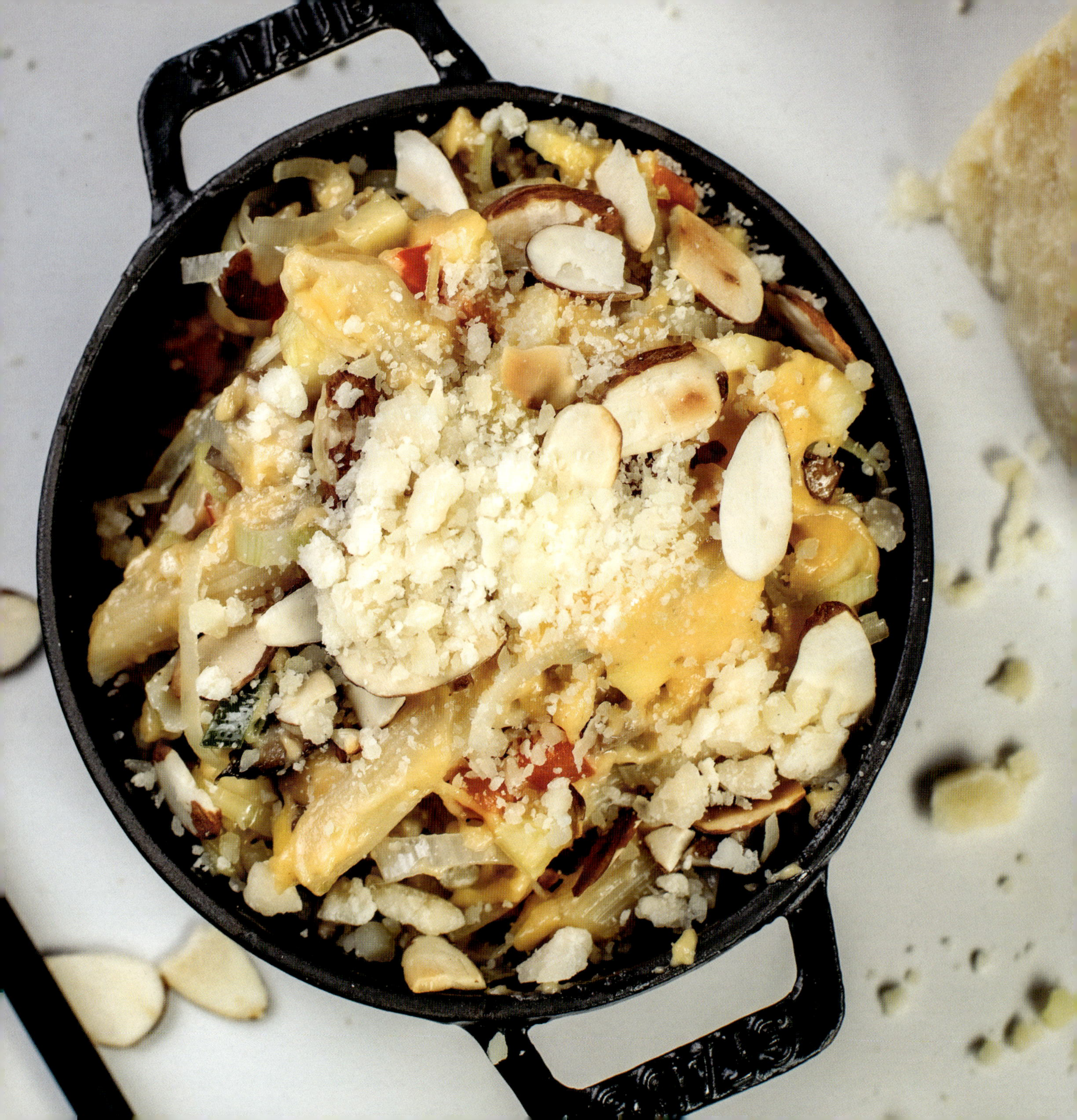

Mac & Cheese & Veg

Prep 15 minutes

Cook 50 minutes

Serves 6-8 servings

Okay, okay, it's mac & cheese, ideal for late night cravings or a quick lunch. But this recipe is so much more. You can make it with any vegetables that you've picked up fresh from a farmers market — or that are sitting in the crisper drawer of your refrigerator. We also like to make this recipe with chickpea or lentil pasta, for an added pinch of protein.

Ingredients

2 cups pasta of your choice, cooked

1 large red bell pepper, diced

1 leek, halved, washed, 1/8 inch slices

1 yellow squash, diced

8 ounces of mushrooms of your choice, diced

3 cloves of garlic

3 Tbsp flour

6 Tbsp infused butter

2 Tbsp fresh thyme leaves

3 cups of 2% milk

2 cups arugula

¼ cup freshly grated Parmesan

1 cup sharp cheddar, Gouda, or other cheese of your choice

1/4 cup of sliced almonds

Preparation

Preheat the oven to 325 degrees F.
Halve and cut the leek into 1/8 inch slices; core and dice the bell pepper, squash, mushrooms, and garlic. Phew!

Toss veggies in a skillet over medium heat with half the infused butter until soft, then add the thyme leaves and cook for 10 minutes. Take off the heat.

For the cheese sauce: in another sauce pan, stir in the infused butter and flour on medium heat and mix until light brown. Add the milk and simmer for 10 more minutes, stirring regularly. Mix in the non-Parmesan cheese until it melts. Season it with salt and pepper. Add arugula, then pulse it all in a blender until smooth.

Put the cooked pasta in a large oven safe casserole dish. Mix the cheese sauce and veggies into the pasta, top with Parmesan and sprinkle the almonds over the top. Pop it in the oven for 30 minutes. Finish in the broiler for 30 seconds for a crispy top layer.

1 Be sure your chicken is room temperature and patted dry inside and out, before tucking in the herbed butter.

2 Trussing the chicken keeps it tucked in tight, so it cooks evenly and stays juicy.

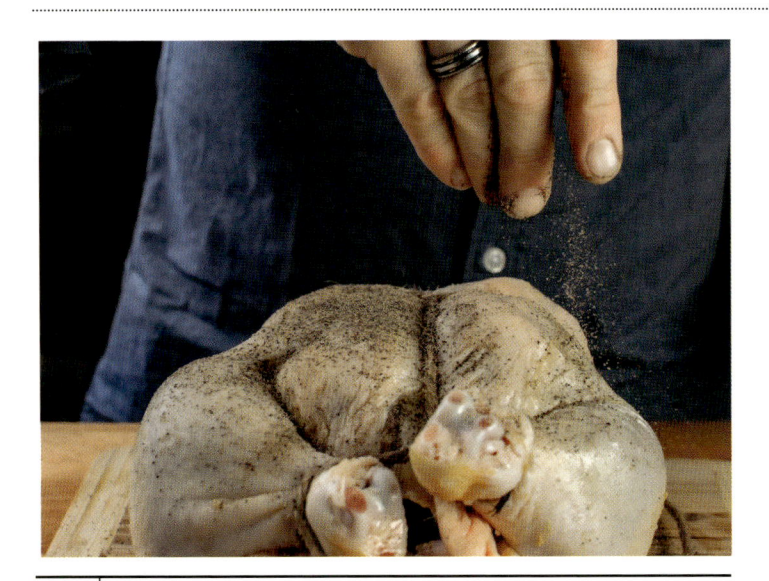

3 Don't be shy with the salt and pepper; the skin will get crunchy, and the meat underneath will taste delicious.

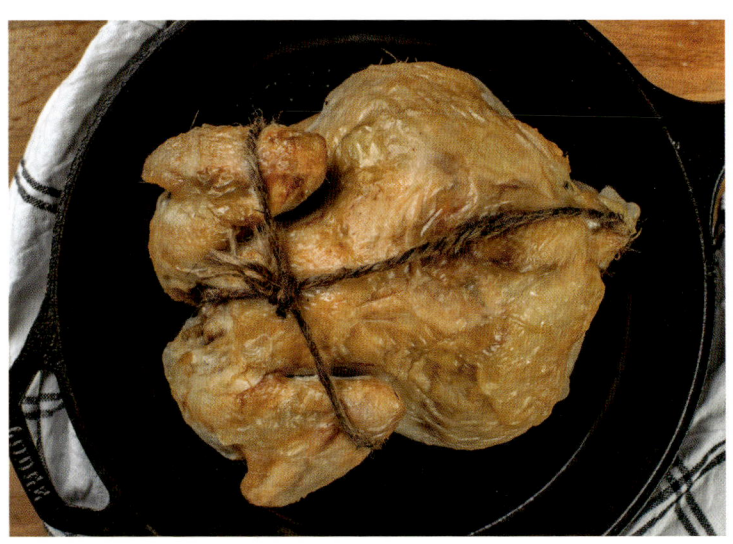

4 Remove and let it sit for 10 minutes before carving.

The Only Roast Chicken You'll Ever Need

They say the greatest test of a chef's ability is their talent roasting chicken. It requires living up to collective nostalgia. Most of us have memories of chicken dishes past, of how the smell fills a home with happy thoughts. This recipe looks simple but needs attention to detail to make sure the meat isn't over- or undercooked. Great with rosemary-garlic infused butter.

Prep 40 minutes

Cook 1 hour 15 min

Serves 6-8 servings

Ingredients

1 small roasting chicken

1 big garlic clove

2 Tbsp shallot, minced

2 tsp fresh thyme

1 Tbsp tarragon, roughly chopped

8 Tbsp infused butter

2 onions

Trussing string

Salt and black pepper

Preparation

Let the chicken come to room temperature for 30 minutes, resisting the urge to wash it off! Washing will trap moisture inside the chicken, making it steam rather than roast. The high heat will cook away any germs.

While it's resting, preheat your oven to 450° F, then blend the garlic, shallot, thyme, tarragon, and parsley or mix them in a mortar and pestle. Add the infused butter and set aside. Next, dry the chicken inside and out with paper towels getting rid of as much moisture as possible. Then, loosen the skin from the surface of the chicken by prying two fingers gently underneath starting near the neck. Push the infused butter mixture between the skin and the meat on the breast side. Then season the chicken inside and out with salt and pepper. Next, truss: tie the ends of both legs so they touch, then criss-cross around the bird vertically and horizontally so the legs and wings are held in tight. Make sure the cavity is closed. This creates a package of savory juiciness. Place the chicken breast-side up in a Dutch oven or other big pot, with 2 rough cut onions underneath to add extra flavor and keep the skin from sticking.

Pop it in the hot oven for 15 minutes, then turn the heat down to 350° and bake for 1 hour, until a meat thermometer registers 160° F in the thickest meat of the thigh. Remove and let it sit for 10 minutes before carving.

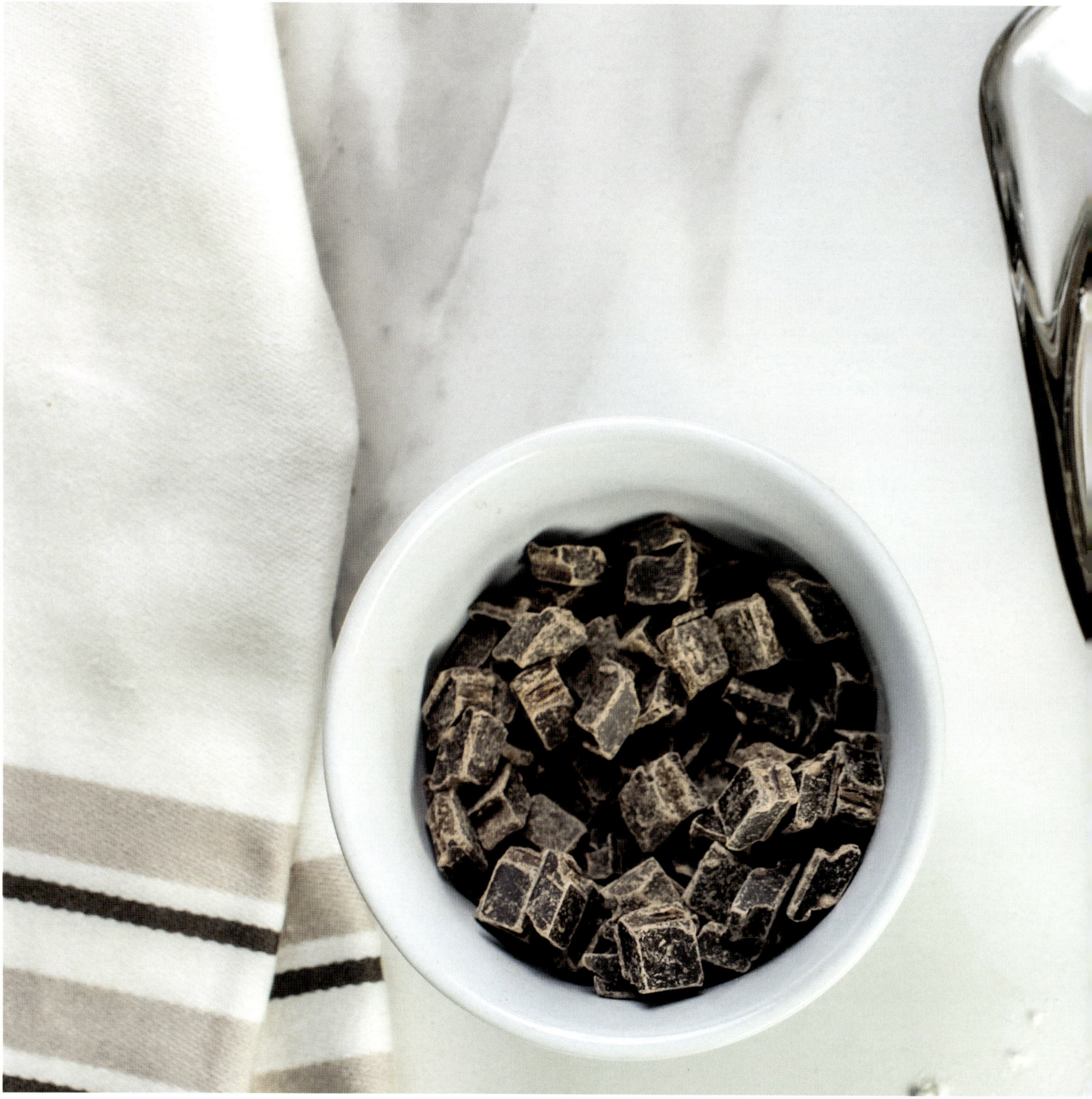

The Munchies

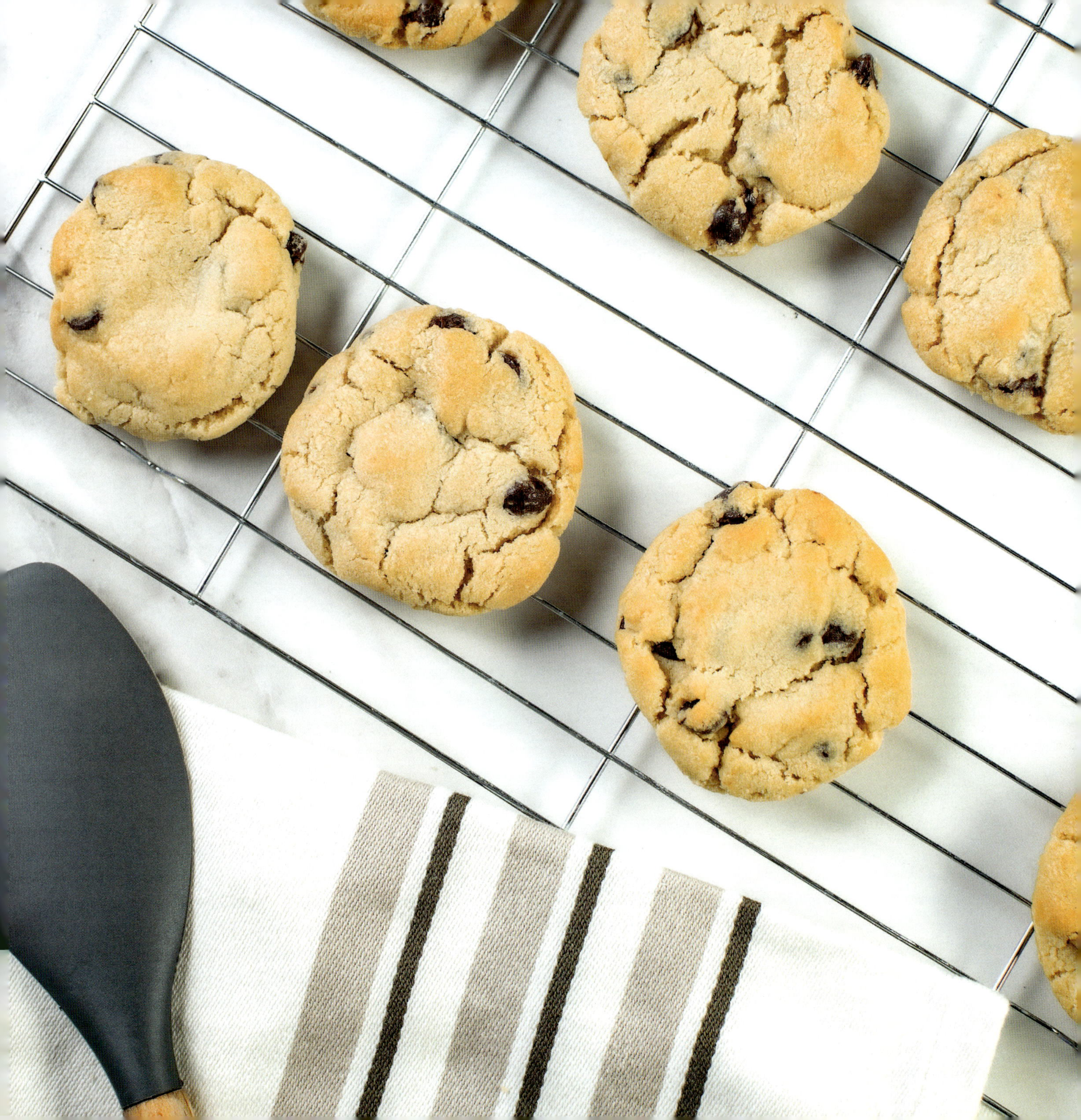

Desserts? Snacks?

Call them what you like, these are delicious doseables, munchies that satisfy the munchies, and whenever that happens we won't judge. Like the author Ernestine Ulmer says, "Life is uncertain. Eat dessert first."

Recipes

- Toll in the House Cookies
- White Chocolate Cheesecake
- Power Gummies
- Coconut Apricot Nugs

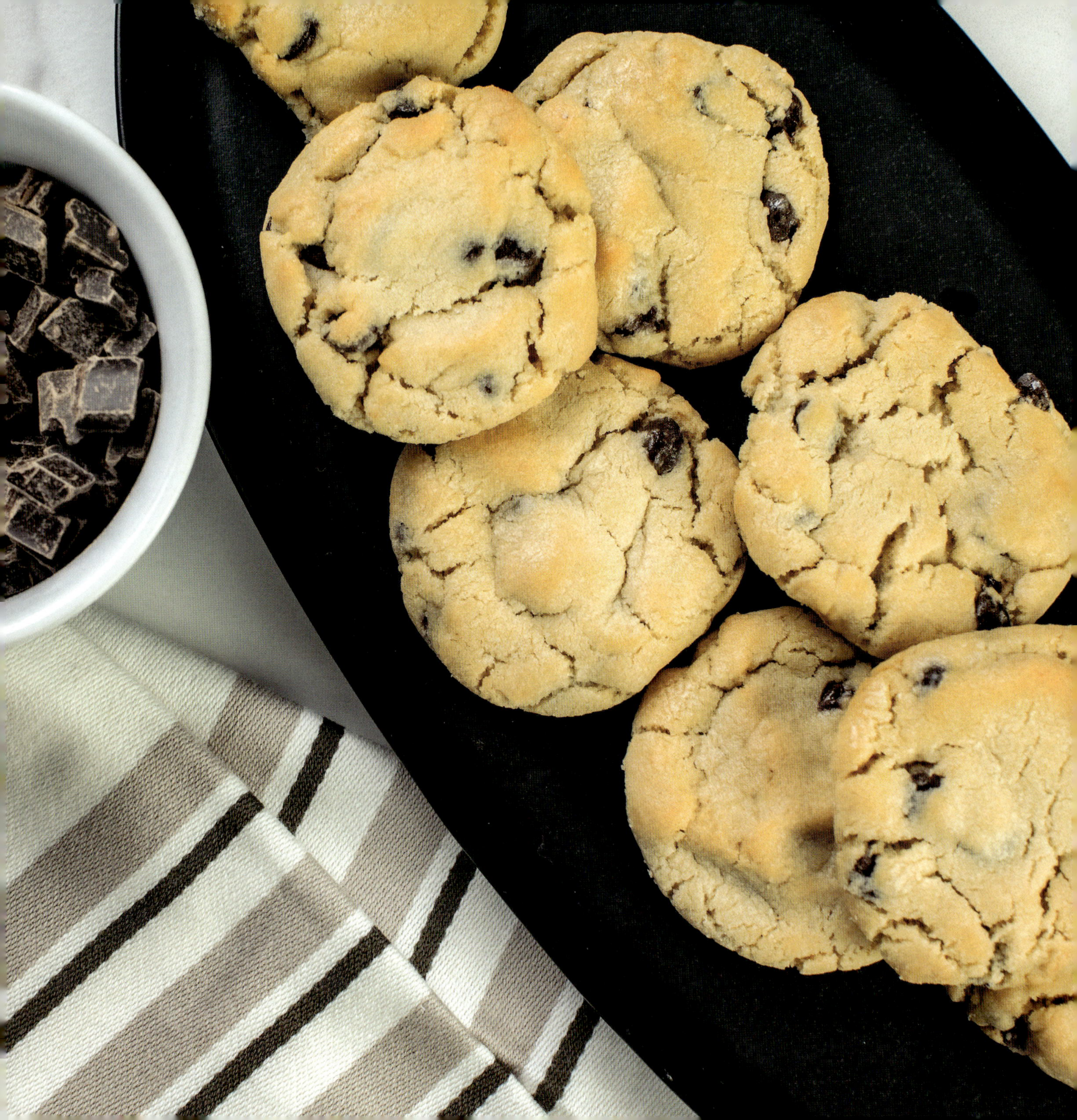

Toll in the House Cookies

Prep 10 minutes

Cook 10 minutes

Serves 3 dozen cookies

We love experimenting with recipes and riffing on classics. But sometimes it's unwise to mess with perfection. No offense to your favorite grandma, but using infused butter will blow her cookies away. Unless your grandma is already down like that, in which case, tell her to give us a call.

Ingredients

2 ¼ cups all purpose flour
1 tsp baking soda
1 tsp salt
1 cup infused butter, softened
¾ cup sugar
¾ cup packed brown sugar
1 tsp bourbon-based vanilla extract
2 large eggs
2 cups semi-sweet chocolate chips

For those who feel nuts:
1 cup walnuts, pecans, or pistachios, stored for 1 week in an airtight container with spices of your choice. We recommend cardamom, nutmeg and star anise.

Preparation

Preheat oven to 375° F. Combine flour, salt, and baking soda in a bowl and set aside.

In a separate bowl, add melted butter, sugar, brown sugar, and vanilla extract.

Mix with a standing mixer, or by hand with a fork until creamy. Add eggs, one at a time, beating well after each addition. Gradually fold in the remaining dry ingredients. Mix in chocolate chips and optional nuts.

Portion each cookie with a rounded Tbsp, drop onto ungreased baking sheets, and bake for around 10 minutes or until golden brown. Cool on a baking sheet for two minutes and eat while warm.

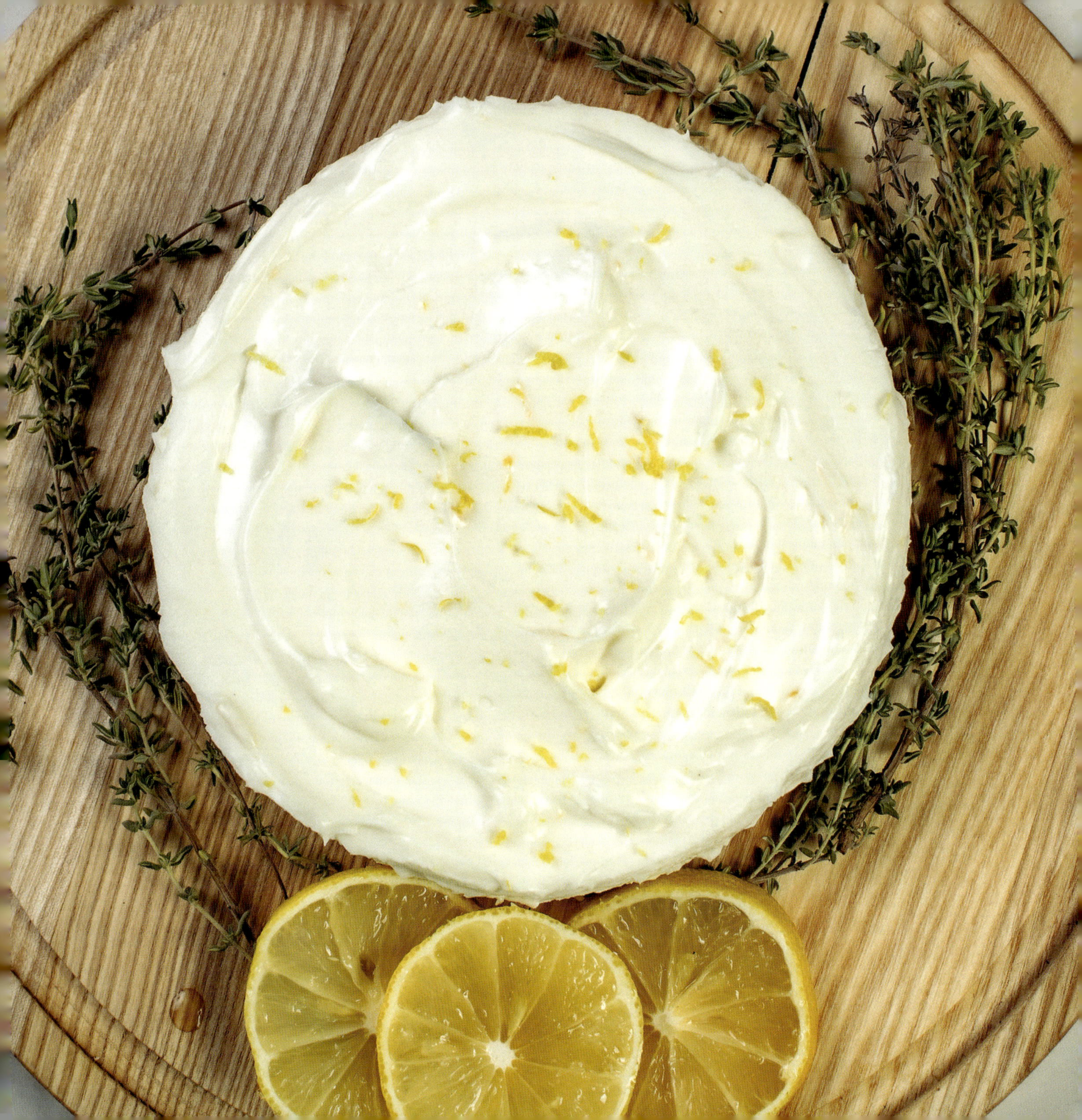

White Chocolate Cheesecake

Prep 30 minutes
Chill 2 hours

Cook 10 minutes

Serves 8 servings

This recipe, like everything inspired by Yotam Ottolenghi, is both gorgeous and delicious. We've tweaked it a bit to make it as easy as possible, spotlight the infused honey, and create a home-baked crust. Trust us, the cookie crumble crust is worth the extra steps and makes this cheesecake a show-stopper.

Ingredients

The Crust

1 egg
1 tsp vanilla extract
4 Tbsp sugar
⅓ cup infused butter, softened
½ tsp baking soda
1 ½ cups of rolled oats, powdered in a food processor
¼ cup unsalted butter, melted
1 Tbsp fresh thyme

The Cheesecake

2 cups no-fat Greek yogurt
14 oz cream cheese
¼ cup powdered sugar
Zest of 1 lemon
5 oz white chocolate, broken & melted
3 Tbsp infused honey

Preparation

For the crust, beat the eggs, vanilla, and sugar together then add softened infused butter and whisk. Fold in the oat flour and baking soda, then roughly spoon "cookies" onto an ungreased baking sheet. Bake for 10 minutes and cool. Pop the cookie crumbles into a clean, dry food processor, mix with the regular butter and thyme leaves. Line the bottom of a 9-inch springform pan with parchment paper and press the crust flat in the bottom.

For the cheesecake: set a clean towel over a bowl and pour the yogurt right into it. Pull the sides of the towel together and squeeze out as much liquid as possible. Whisk the yogurt with the cream cheese, powdered sugar, and lemon zest until smooth. Melt the white chocolate in a heatproof glass bowl over a saucepan of gently simmering water (don't let the bottom of the bowl touch the water, or the chocolate will burn). Stir as it melts, then fold it into the yogurt mixture and whisk.

Spread over the crust and refrigerate for 2 hours. Drizzle with infused honey and sprinkle with extra thyme.

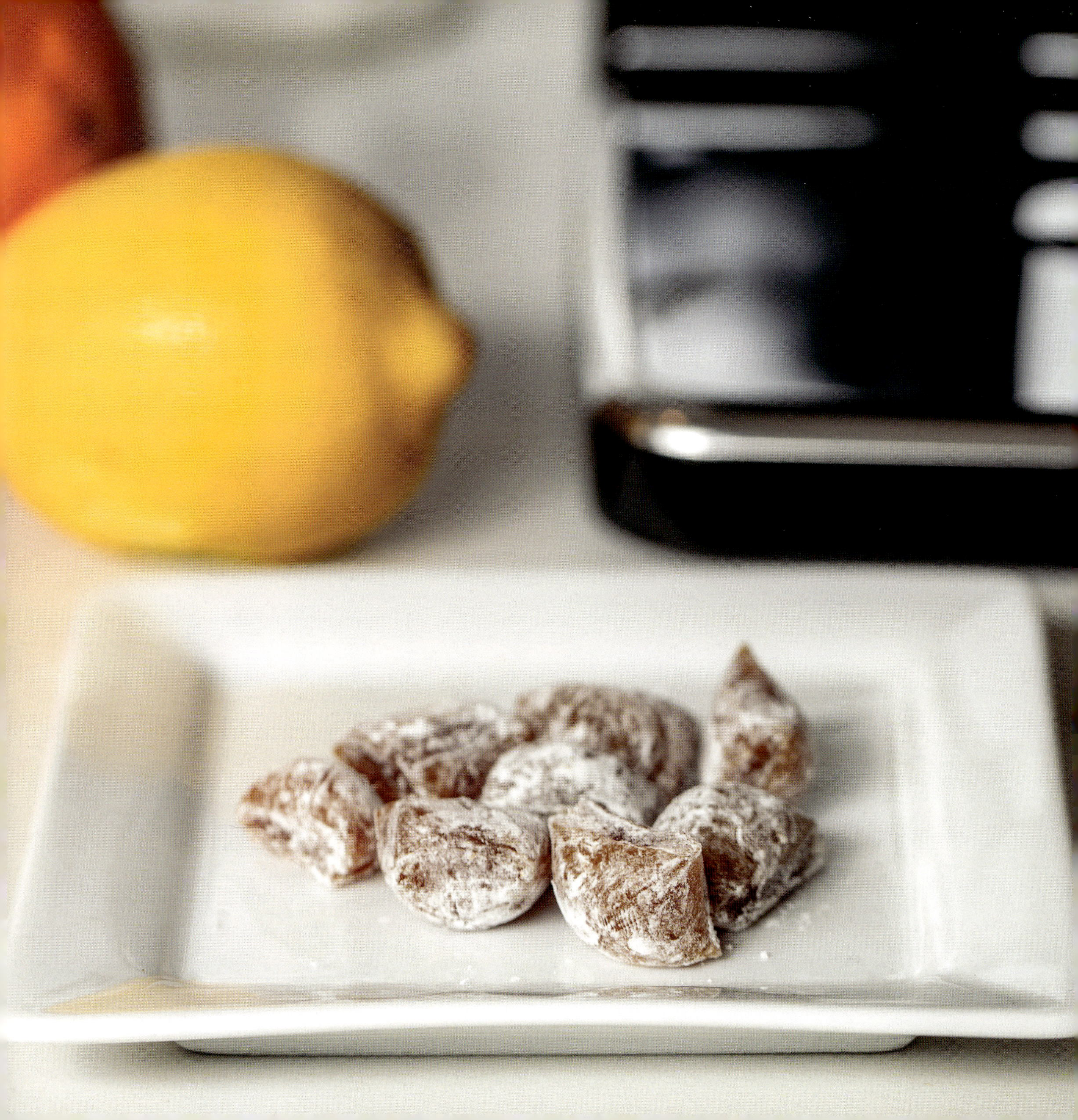

Power Gummies

Prep 20 minutes

Serves 24 gummies

The almighty gummy. Even if you're not a Flintstone prepare to get bedrocked. There are as many gummy recipes out there as there are colors of the rainbow, but we've created one that's super simple, delicious, and packs a real (fruit) punch.

Ingredients

16 oz package of your favorite flavor of Jello-O, Royal Gelatin, Jolly Rancher Gelatin or generic gelatin mix

1 ½ cups freshed squeezed orange juice

½ cup infused honey

¼ cup infused coconut oil

4 packets unflavored gelatin

Cornstarch to sprinkle

Preparation

Mix the flavored gelatin with 1 cup of orange juice in a saucepan over low heat.

Once it's combined, add the infused honey and infused oil, constantly whisking.

With your free hand (or a cooking colleague), mix all four packs of unflavored gelatin with the rest of the orange juice in a bowl and let it sit for 5 minutes. Add the juice-gelatin mixture into the saucepan and keep cooking over low heat for 5 minutes. Don't stop whisking! Be sure to scrape the sides and bottom so none of the mixture burns.

Portion into LĒVO silicone Gummy Molds with the droppers provided, working quickly as it will start setting right away.

Let them cool completely on the counter, then put them into the fridge. Let set for at least 1 hour, then pop them out of the tray into a bowl.

Sprinkle them all over with corn starch, to keep from sticking to each other, and store in an airtight container in the fridge.

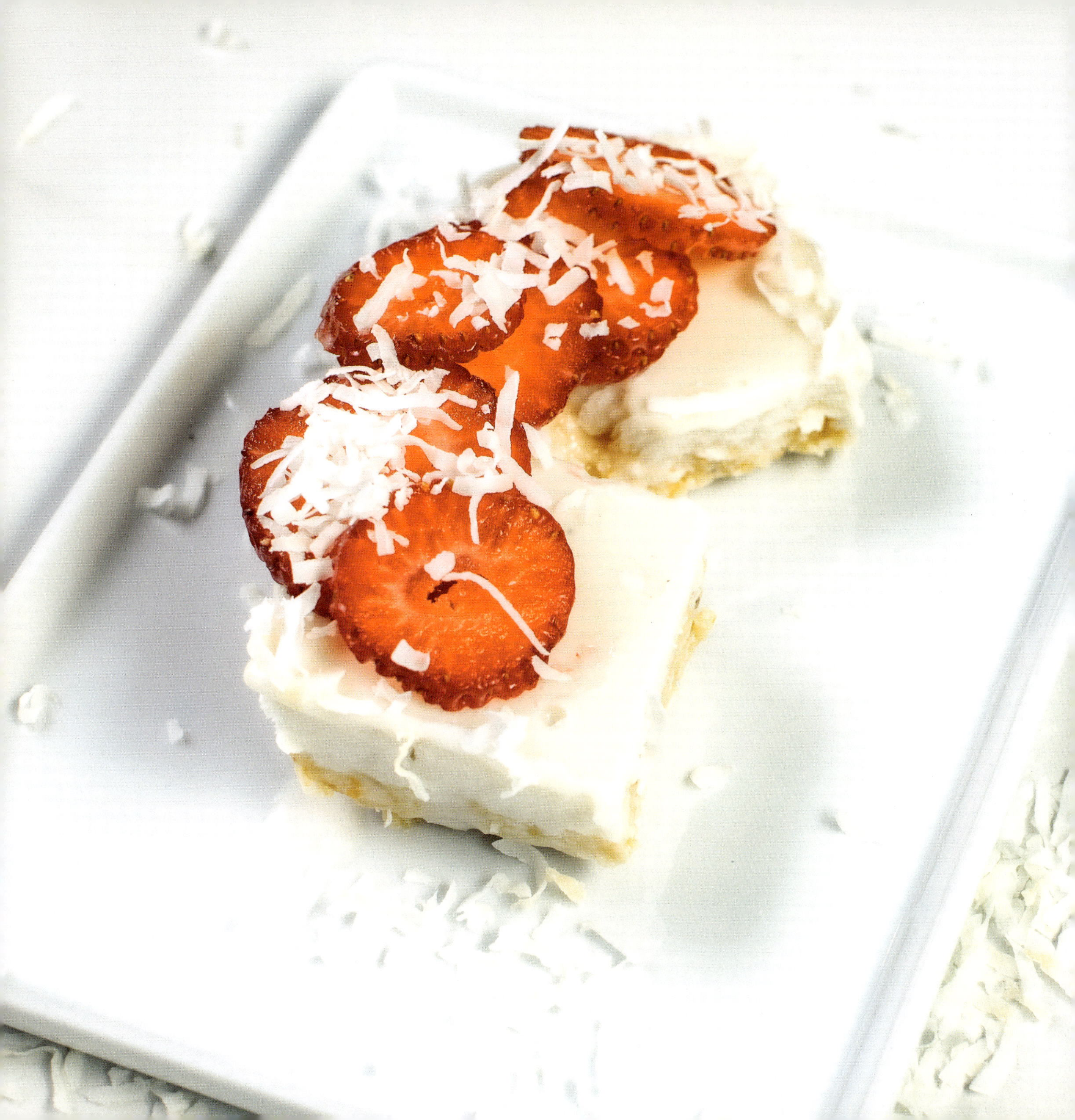

Coconut Apricot Nugs

Prep 20 minutes

Chill crust 30 minutes
Chill topping 2 hours

Serves 12 nugs

Remember no-bake desserts? Don't call it a comeback, call it a dessert treat that puts a smile on your face and a chill in your stride. All the flavor, but entirely vegan.

Ingredients

1 ½ cups roasted and salted cashews
3 cups of canned coconut cream
1 cup dried apricots
½ tsp cardamon
⅓ cup infused honey
⅓ cup freshly squeezed lemon juice
1 tsp bourbon-based vanilla extract
Freshly sliced strawberries (optional)
1 cup unsweetened shredded coconut

Preparation

Line a 7" x 11" baking dish with parchment paper.

In a food processor, combine cashews, half of the coconut cream, apricots, and cardamom. Pulse until a ball forms. Press it flat into the baking pan: this is your base crust, so make sure it's well packed.

Chill in the refrigerator for 30 minutes.

Next, heat the infused honey and remaining coconut cream in a medium saucepan over medium-high heat. When it starts to boil, reduce and simmer for 10 minutes, then remove from the heat and whisk in the lemon juice, vanilla, and a dab of salt.

Pour the mixture onto the crust, cover, and chill for 2 hours. Serve chilled and top with sliced strawberries and shredded coconut.

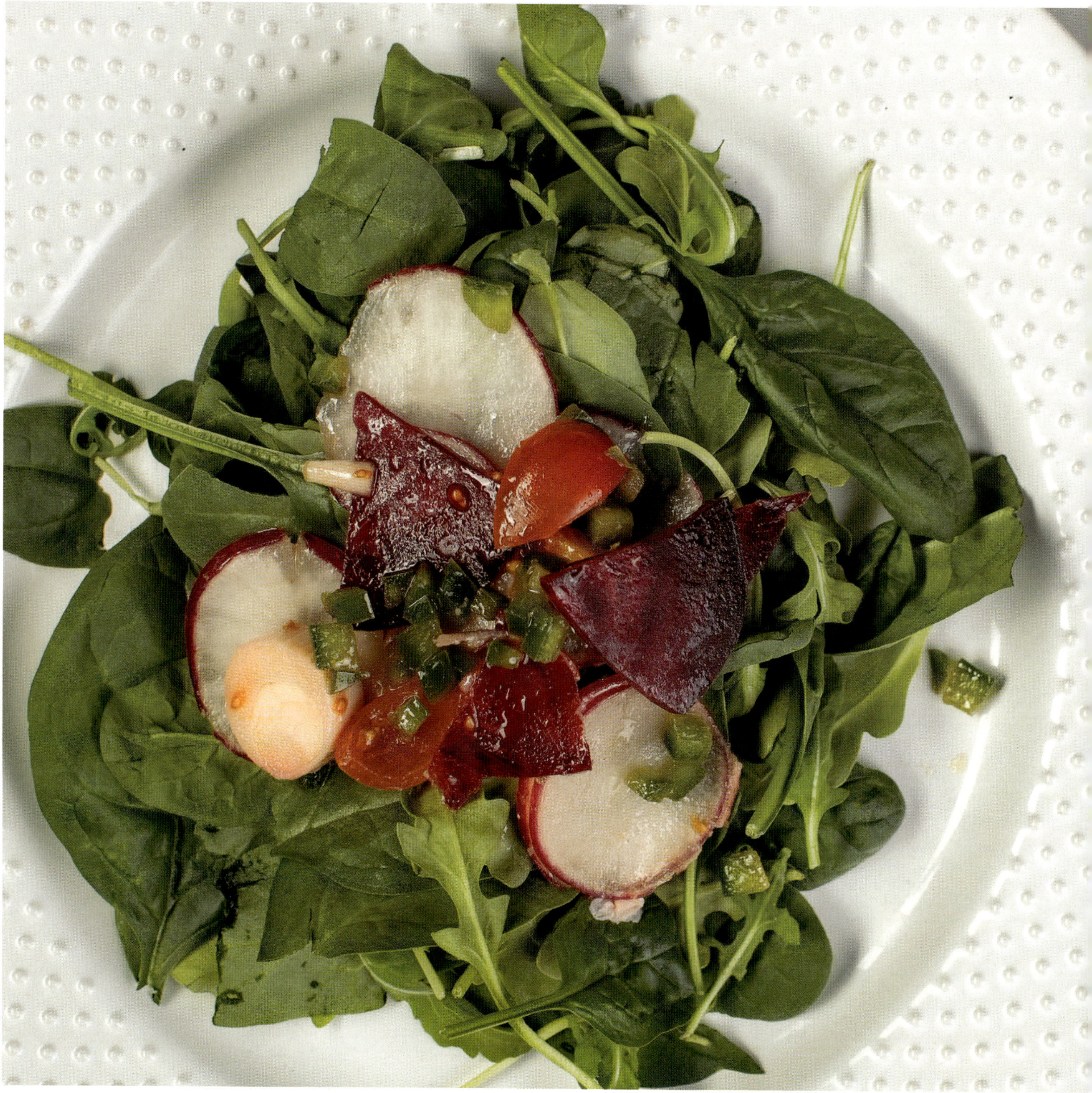

Get Your Fixins

Dressings & Cocktails

The Basic B

Our classic salad dressing and marinade. You might just need to quadruple this recipe when you see how versatile and tasty it is.

Ingredients

1 shallot, minced
1 clove of garlic, minced
½ cup infused olive oil
¼ cup balsamic vinegar
1 tsp infused honey
Freshly ground salt and black pepper to taste

Prep 10 minutes

Serves ¾ cup total liquid

Frenchy Vinaigrette

A tangy option that pairs beautifully with bitter leaves like arugula and endive, or salads with meat, beans, eggs, or potatoes.

Ingredients

1 lemon, freshly squeezed
2 Tbsp Dijon mustard
3 Tbsp infused olive oil
½ Tbsp apple cider vinegar
Freshly ground salt and black pepper, to taste

Prep 10 minutes

Serves ½ cup total liquid

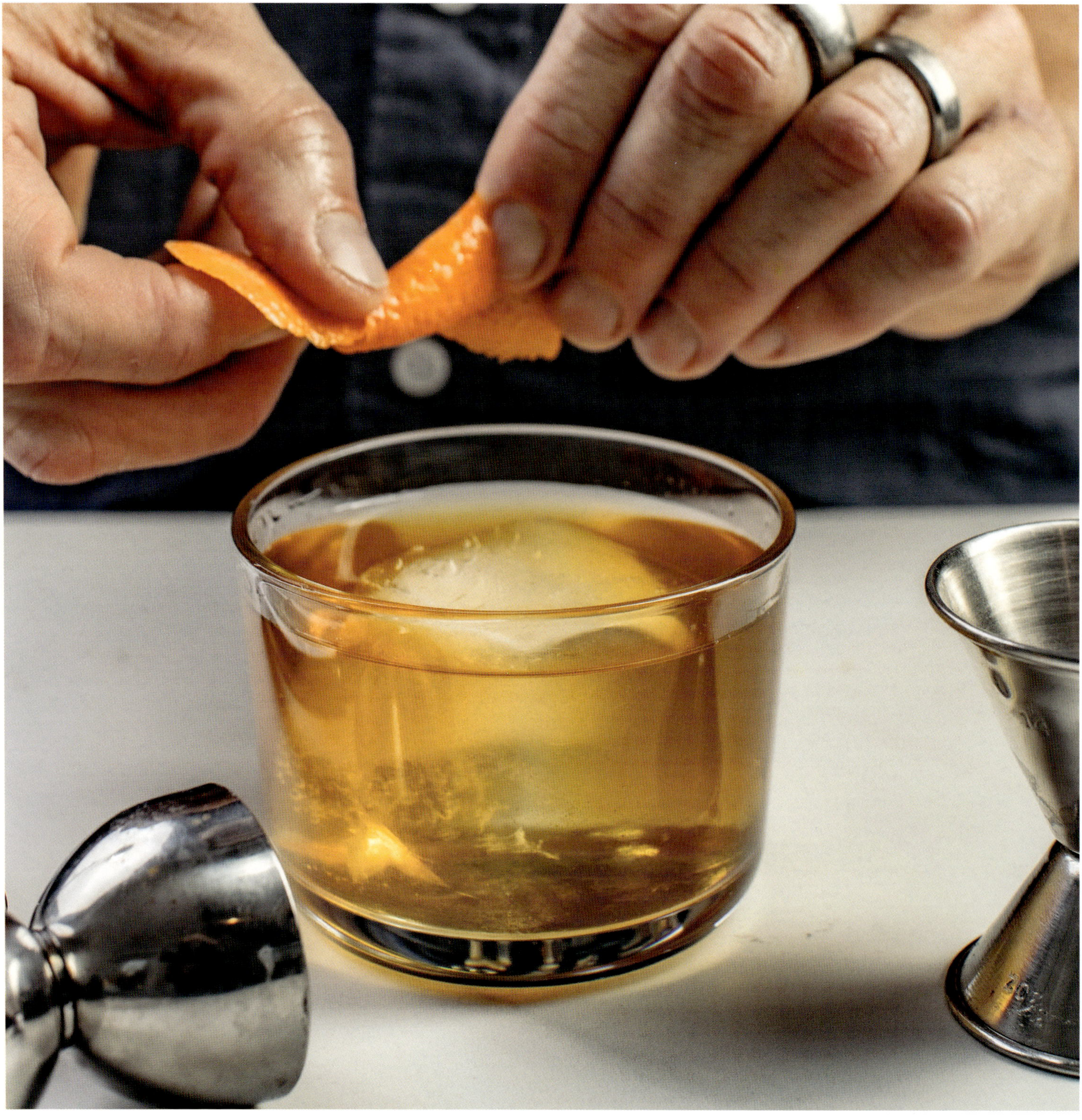

Cocktails

Fat-Washed Cocktails

A savory, silky twist, fat washing started in the mid-aughts at New York's fabled speakeasy Please Don't Tell, with a Benton's bacon-infused Old Fashioned. You don't have to use bacon fat: any oil or butter works beautifully in any drink from a Bloody Mary to a Negroni. Or, drink the fat-infused spirit neat.

Ingredients

1 oz infused butter or fat
12 oz spirit of your choice
2 pint-size mason jars
Cheesecloth
Funnel

Preparation

Infuse into your base of choice, like bacon fat. Once the infusion has run its course, pour the infused base into one of the mason filled with the spirit, seal and shake.

Let it sit for 3-4 hours, then freeze until all of the fat solidifies in a layer at the top.

Scrape out the fat, then strain the spirit through a cheesecloth-lined funnel into the clean jar.

Old Fashioned

Ingredients

2 oz bacon fat-infused bourbon
½ oz simple syrup
2 dashes Angostura bitters
Orange twist

Martini

Ingredients

2 oz fat-washed gin
1 oz sherry
¾ oz olive brine
Lemon peel, expressed over the finished drink then discarded
3 olives, for garnish

Thank You

We hope you're able to take your herbal infusions to new heights with these fun and healthy recipes.

Put your infüsiasm on display by showing us your LĒVO unboxing experience and your favorite herbal creations.

Tag your photos, videos, and special recipes with @levo_oil on Instagram or @levooil on TikTok, and in your caption use the hashtag #LĒVOmade. We love to see LĒVO recipes come to life!

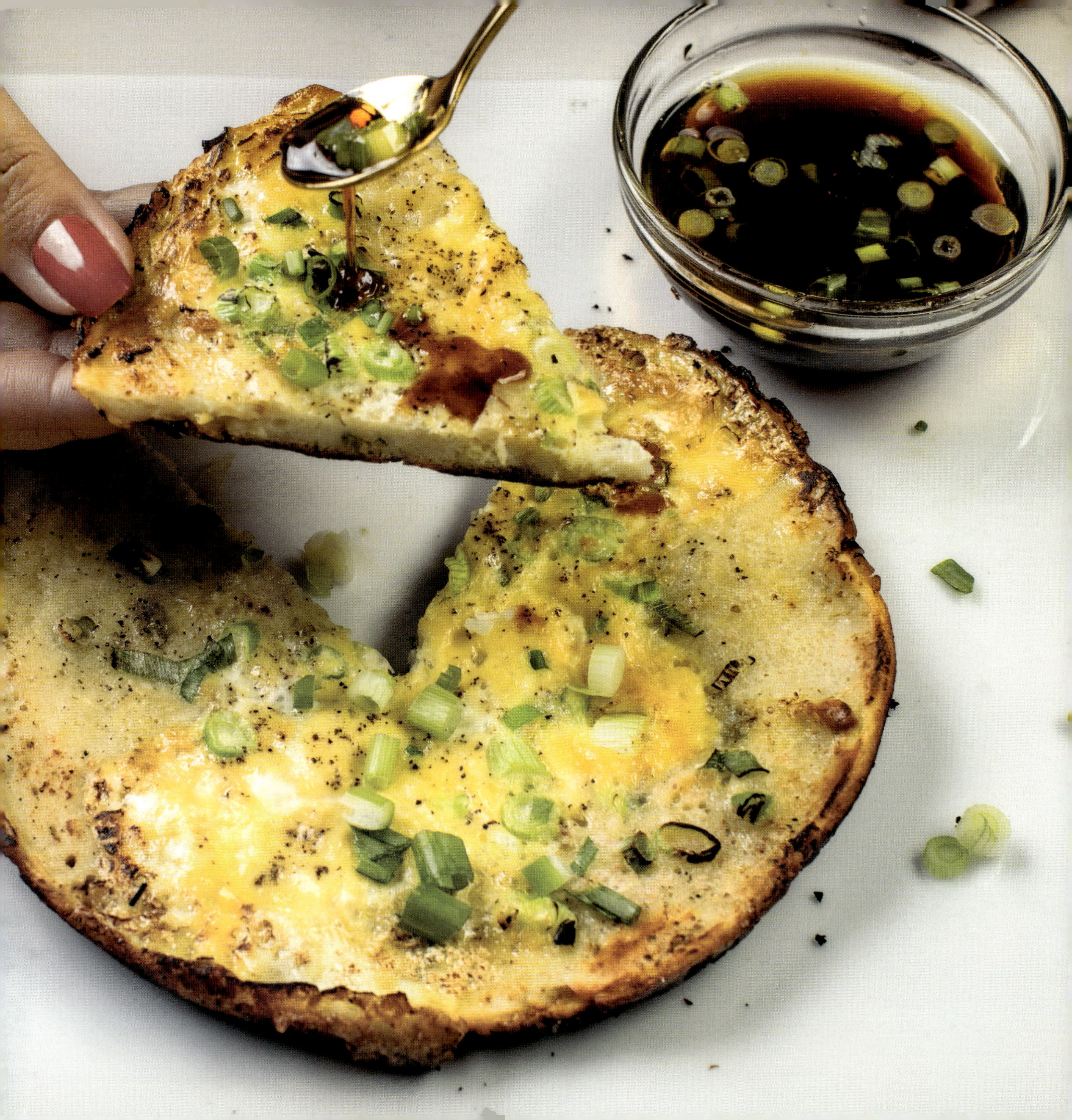

Copyright © 2021 by LĒVO Oil Infusion
All rights reserved. No portion of this book may be reproduced
- mechanically, electronically, or by any other means, including
photocopying - without written permission of the publisher except
for the use of quotations in a book review.

Printed in the USA
First paperback edition July 2021
ISBN 978-1-7365587-2-0
eISBN 978-1-7365587-0-6

For more recipes and to purchase LĒVO and accessories
used in this book, visit us online at levooil.com
For specific questions, contact us at support@levooil.com

LĒVO Oil Infusion
66 S Logan St
Denver, CO
80209